COUNTRY TALES
OLD
GAMEKEEPERS

ooooo

Brian P. Martin

D1355429

DAVID & CHARLES

Cover photographs: (front) by Felix Man © Hulton Getty;
(back) supplied by the author

The material in this book was originally published in a fuller form
under the titles *Tales of the Old Gamekeepers* (David & Charles, 1989) and
More Tales of the Old Gamekeepers (David & Charles, 1993)

A DAVID & CHARLES BOOK

First published in the UK in 1998

A catalogue record for this book is available from the British Library.

ISBN 0 7153 0835 1

Printed in the UK by Mackays of Chatham plc
for David & Charles
Brunel House   Newton Abbot   Devon

CONTENTS

INTRODUCTION

———— ooooo ————

The reminiscences of men aged 55 to 100 comprise the nucleus of this book, and if there is one thing my research has taught me it is respect for my elders; and this experience has impressed upon me just how fleeting are man's years on this ever-changing earth. At the same time I have been surprised how sharp the memory of boyhood can remain down the long years. Of course, we all remember the milestones and important dates in our lives, but I doubt if many people can recapture the details of old English country life as these men have.

Men have always said that, like the poet, the keeper is born and not made, and in this a certain amount of truth still remains. The basic qualities required have always been great loyalty, genuine concern for fellow men and a detailed knowledge and love of the countryside and natural history. But early keepering was often an extension of serfdom in which the under-privileged worked incredibly hard to satisfy the whims of sometimes ungrateful and ignorant masters. Fortunately, we have come far this century and at long last most keepers do not need to touch their forelocks quite so much. The subjects of my books have witnessed tremendous improvements in pay and conditions of service, but they have often had to fight every inch of the way to overcome the pomposity and selfishness of a minority who have literally inherited the earth.

One thing that has remained constant has been the gamekeeper's standing in the country community – friend of prince and pauper and the confidant of everyone, enjoying the respect

5

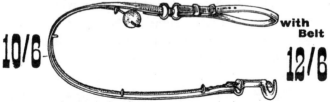

of both humble village folk and landed gentry. More than once has a famous politician sought the honest opinion of his keeper on some sensitive public or private issue, and often has the farm labourer turned to his friend the keeper in his hour of need. In no other occupation has a man ever needed to get on with so many people from all walks of life.

The commitment of the old-time keeper was total – 365 days a year and often twenty-four hours a day in all weathers, night-watching or on the rearing field, with the constant threat of injury or even death at the hands of vicious poachers. Before the advent of the motor car, access to the majority of shoots in remote rural areas was difficult, so most poachers were local men with whom the keeper played a perpetual game of cat and mouse. And in dealing with many poor people struggling to support large families he did have some sympathy. But today all is different and the old-fashioned 'one-for-the-pot' man has been replaced by highly mobile gangs of thugs who stop short of nothing. It was inevitable that tales of poaching should occupy so many of these pages, but they do illustrate very well the evolution of society's attitude towards offenders. In this, as in everything, I have let the keepers tell the tales in their own words wherever possible.

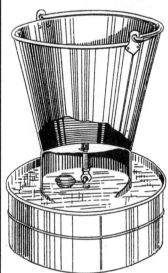

SURVIVOR OF THE TRENCHES

———————— ooooo ————————

When 19-year-old gamekeeper Ned Turvey volunteered for the Army in World War I he was completely unaware of the carnage which lay ahead of him. Seventy-eight years later, at the age of ninety-seven, he remained a firm believer in discipline and reflected on the sad decline of the old-fashioned virtues which helped him survive both the terror of the trenches and a lifetime in keepering.

One of seven children, Edward Victor Randolph Turvey (always known as Ned) was born on 20 September 1895, at Hilton Park, near Wolverhampton, where his father was headkeeper for twelve years.

At the age of three and a half, Ned went to Essington School – 'all galvanised sheeting, just like the church. We used to walk through the woods to get there. I had a good, firm master. People used to say, "Mr Walker's a very good man – he goes to church on Sunday and prays to the Lord to give him strength to wallop the kids on Monday". Parents don't bother with their children now. It's all too easy.

'Owing to ill health in the family, the doctor advised my parents to leave the house, so in 1900 we moved to Lord Hatherton's estate, between Cannock and Penkridge, where father was again headkeeper.

'Father was a good provider and we was a happy family. We always went to church and Sunday school and was taught things properly. There was always a rabbit or pigeon to eat and you always had a good garden. Mother was a tiptop cook too – been in gentlemen's service. We 'ad a lot of good soup then and plenty of good bacon. All meat was no price: hip-bone steak just 10d (4p) a pound and sausages 4d a pound – none of these fancy prices now. Meat was much tastier too, with a little bit of fat – that's what you want! Mother always knew what to buy – she 'ad to as there was nine of us in the house with a keeper lodgin'.

'Years ago a lad used to bring out the Guns' lunches from Paterson's at Birmingham – everythin' you could want. Then my wife took over, and everybody loved mother's damson jam. Before the first war father used to get Flower's best bitter delivered from Penkridge for 10d a gallon. Even the very best bitter was only shilling a gallon. It came on the train, then the local grocer brought it out.

'Then there was plenty of wildlife of every description, including corncrakes, nightjars and quails. 'Course the vermin was kept down and that made the difference. There it is – the law of the land. And the woods was magnificent with bluebells and daffodils. I remember years later, when they cut all the trees down, I've never seen such a pretty sight as all the foxgloves.'

Ned never had any secret ambition while still in education and it was no surprise when he left school, at the age of thirteen years and four months in 1908, to work with his father. 'Everythin' was dead against you then, and in the keeperin' world at least you very soon learned that a still tongue was a wise tongue.'

Without motorised transport in relatively isolated rural communities, Ned and his generation rapidly learned to become self-sufficient. And as the doctor had to be paid for his services, many folk had their own remedies for various ailments. Ned certainly stuck by his. Indeed, as we spoke he noticed that I was looking distinctly uncomfortable because my long car journey had aggravated a back complaint. 'I reckon you've got a touch of lumbago there', he said. 'I've got a good cure for that – always carry a lump of nutmeg about in your pocket. I've got a little bit on me now.' And with that he reached deep into his trousers pocket to produce a little cloth bag, the drawstring of which he unravelled with some difficulty to reveal a piece of nutmeg worn smooth with the years. 'I can guarantee that if ever I forget it I get twinges. 'Course me father had it very bad.'

Ned's starting pay was seven shillings a week and he was general dogsbody for dad and two other keepers. 'After the main shooting was over I had to get two gallons of paraffin from a shop in the village, soak pieces of sacking, light them and drop 'em down holes to stink the rabbits out. 'Course you 'ad a lighted piece with you all the time as there was no matches. This took me about a week, then the Guns had a day's shooting and killed about 150 rabbits.

'Shooting was a real pleasure then – everybody was happy. I remember one time a Gun's hat blew off and 'e said "Don't worry, my dog will fetch it". Instead of that the dog buried it and we all had a jolly good laugh. It were the sort of thing that made a day. No one was bothered about these huge bags then.

'In my young days all the shooting was walkin' the fields with the Guns in line through the roots. Partridges were everywhere and there were lots of hares. But it could be dangerous and if you got your dog lost that was the end of it till 'e was found.

'When I was sixteen I took a chap's beat and became under-keeper, with full responsibility for a 140-acre wood at Penkridge. Altogether we reared about 2,500 pheasants and there were traps all over the place then. The hedgehog was the worst vermin on a partridge beat. We 'ad to 'ave pole traps for the brown owl – they was very destructive, but I did protect the white owl.

'We bought some eggs, but plenty was picked-up along the roadsides. Then the roads was just rough stones rolled in and when a car went by you saw the dust for hell of a while after.'

In January 1915 Ned joined the 8th South Staffordshire Regiment, 17th Division. 'We went to Lichfield Barracks for five days, then they put sixty of us on the trains and sent us down to Bovington Camp in Dorset. There we 'ad lots of bayonet practice and route marchin' round Tolpuddle and all about. But I took it all in me stride – we went to serve king and country and thought it'd all be over by Christmas. I met some very decent people, very decent, and in England the food was good.'

After two months Ned was sent to Lulworth Cove, where the men were under canvas. 'In April they ordered us to bathe in the sea, but it was too damn cold and we very soon put our clothes on. A month later we marched to Winchester to Flower Down Camp, to fire our course over the range.' There certainly wasn't much regard for human dignity in the Army then, as Ned bitterly recalls. 'Outside Winchester we all had to line up naked for a medical along the roadside. Anybody could 'ave come along and seen us.

'By golly there were some mugs with rifles there, but we got by. After a short time we got on the train at Basingstoke and went to Dover, then crossed to Boulogne. They took us up in cattle trucks to St Omer and then we had to march the rest of the way, to a place called St Eloi. We were there seventeen days – went in spick and span and came out lousy as the Devil – just holdin' the line. We had a very good officer for our platoon, S.R. Edwards from Sussex, a grand chap who had the men's interest at heart. He wanted me to be a sniper, which I didn't want. Anyway, he didn't last ten days in the trenches as a shell killed him by my side – 'ad his head half cut right off.

'Then I took up stretcher-bearing and as Lance-Corporal I 'ad eight men under me. This lasted for two and a half years until the regiment was broken up with losses. I was then transferred to the 7th South Staffordshire Regiment, 11th Division. We travelled most parts of the line. It was all bad and dangerous and we got down ready for the Somme advance.

'In July 1916 we started at a place called Fricourt village, where we were rushed after another regiment had been in and got cut up badly. We hadn't been in the trenches long when I heard a shout for help, in no man's land. It was a German officer with a fractured femur, but he was not bleeding. I got some more stretcher-bearers across and we took him to the doctors' dug-out. We always treated everybody the same. Then he pulled his platinum ring off and gave it to me. Since then I have passed the ring on to my granddaughter.

'We then went to Delville Wood to hold on to it after the South Africans had been carved up. I was told there was a man in front wounded, so I crawled forward in the daylight to help him. I was about fifty yards out in no man's land and calling as quietly as I could when I felt a crack on my back. It was a sniper cut my webbing belt off with a bullet. Anyway I couldn't find the man and thought he had been shot so I crawled back into the trenches.

'Next day I had another lucky escape when a shell killed two men in the trench within three yards of me. But everyone had that risk. We wrapped 'em up in oil cloth and took 'em down to the road for collection, but they were still just layin' there a week after when we came away. Your groundsheet was your coffin then.

'I spent my 21st birthday on the Somme, at Hebetune. Mother sent me a chicken and a plum puddin' and four of us ate it all that night. By golly that were a good change. All we had to drink was the water brought up in petrol cans, but the food helped us forget the thousands of rats, which 'ad many a carcass there.

'When I finished stretcher-bearing I was made the sergeant of a platoon, towards the end of the war. And when the big push came it was all over. I happened to be home on leave when armistice was declared. My sister got married at exactly the same time – 11am on 11 November 1918 – at Penkridge church, and I was best man. Then I was transferred back to France and eventually returned to England and Hatherton Hall in February 1919. Then I really 'ad to start work.'

While Ned had been away his father had suffered two serious illnesses, 'So the place was run down, well poached with ferrets and whippets and overrun with vermin. But I soon got busy and gave the poachers and pests a tannin', which is not done today! For each case proved I 'ad 3/6d off the magistrates' clerk – it all came out of costs, so the poachers paid. And if one man had a gun they 'ad the others for aidin' and abettin'. 'Course, the police were different then – great big chaps too.

'I always 'ad a damn good staff [stick] and most of the time the poachers 'ad only got to see it. But sometimes I 'ad a battle royal. Some gypsies came in once – they'd been drinkin'. I sent my son to tell 'em to go, but they didn't so I went up. There were three vans of 'em. I said, "Come on, off you go". Then one struck at me and I 'it 'im with me truncheon on the head and the blood really fled. But I was sorry for him. Then another came on, but I 'ad 'im too and then they cleared off.

'There were a tremendous amount of gypsies about in them days. You were supposed to get the police in to move 'em on. As well as game they took wood for pegs and even ferns to sell. To help catch the poachers we used to set a stuffed cock pheasant by the road and watch for them to come for it.'

In 1931 two of the shooting syndicate died and Ned's father retired. Ned took over as headkeeper for a new syndicate. 'Me pay went up from about 35 bob to £2 a week, rent and rates were free and I had a ton of coal and a suit of clothes a year.'

When World War II came along Ned was exempt from service as he was in charge of a small acreage and required to keep the vermin down and grow crops. 'In any case there was no way I was goin' in that bloody lot again! Feeding the birds was not allowed then but sometimes I 'ad the puggins [tail-end corn] to keep the pheasants together.'

The winter of 1940–1 was very hard. 'The snow blocked us in for six weeks. That's what we're short of now – there's never any snow water to fill the passages up. We only 'ad a small skitterin' this last time [winter 1991–2]. Not like 1947 – that were a damn bad 'un. In the April we went down to Ilfracombe for a while so that Alice could rest after a serious illness, and there was sheep lyin' dead all over the place.'

Family holidays were always by train as Ned never owned a car. 'One of the gents was goin' to give me one once, but 'e died. It were tough for the toffs too when taxation got in and then they weren't so liberal. In the old days you always 'ad yer £5 Christmas Box on Boxing Day and that were somethin' then. Sometimes people did 'ave a golden sovereign, but never once did I 'ave a £5 tip, not like today when a tenner is looked down on.'

After 1940 no rearing was done, the woods were cut down and Ned worked for various shooting tenants on his own up to retirement in 1962, by which time he had served the 3,500-acre estate for fifty-four years – his entire working life apart from war service.

While Ned lamented many changes in keepering he never became embittered and retained a keen interest in everything around him. In his late nineties his main regret was that he could no longer tend the garden which had kept him so active. 'They told me I wouldn't last a six-month when I retired, but I took up mole poisonin', and I'd always do a day's beating when I could. Now this sherry's the finest thing to keep me going.'

Very sadly, Ned Turvey died in February 1993. God bless you Ned – the whole of the civilised world owes you a great debt.

A PROPER
YORKSHIREMAN

———— ooooo ————

Even along the Pennines, where chill winds have bred a tough race, few people are more outspoken than 85-year-old Newton Hutchinson. Proudly he describes himself as, 'a proper Yorkshireman'. Yet no one could take offence at his colourful language because the ever-present twinkle in his eyes reveals the great kindness and friendliness for which Dalesmen are also renowned.

Newton was born on 28 June 1913, at Arkengarthdale, Reeth, near Richmond. At first he lived with his grandfather, who was a miner, but was greatly influenced by his gamekeeper uncle. And he was always close to the land because, 'in those days all miners and most keepers 'ad a bit of ground, with a cow. That was the wife's living. And every garden 'ad vegetables in. Now when I go back it surprises me to see all the roses.

'We never 'ad a lot, but we managed to eat quite well. The butcher came out once a week with 'is pony and trap. Then the farmers used to keep these wee, "shot", unsaleable lambs and when one was killed it was divided up between everyone. Also, grandad always kept a pig or two – everyone did.

'Everybody in the dale could put their hand to somethin' and me ol' grandad was specially good at killin' a pig. This was generally on a Monday because it was washday for a farmer's wife and she already 'ad the copper on for the scaldin' and cleanin' up after. Pig-killin' day was a real friendly do. They always 'ad

17

these five-gallon kegs of beer so they was 'appy as pigs in China.

'Grandad cured the pigs, and made all the sausages an' all. In those days a farmer's wife would send a lad up to you with a big hanky tied round a plate with bits of all the meats off the pig on it. That was her sign of friendship. There was only one feller used to grumble, and 'e was the butcher!

'There were about eighty-four of us children at school, from all over Arkengarthdale. It was big families in them days.' However, Newton was one of only three children. 'My brother Nigel became a keeper on Reeth moors and my sister went to Newcastle to work in munitions.

'The school bus was one of only two motor vehicles in the dale and it took children who lived over three miles away, but I was bloody unlucky because I was two and three-quarter miles off and told to walk. But one of the two drivers was a grand feller and would always pick us up anyway.

'Our two school-teachers were very strict, but I was always a little devil. I never used to go when I was sent for the stick, which was a lot. I just used to go out in the porch, rub my hands and come back pretendin' to cry. But I was found out in the end when the teachers compared notes.'

Unfortunately, the lure of the wild was too much for Newton to bear. 'If I knew they were off foxing I'd put my hand up and say, "Please sir, can I leave the room?" Then as soon as I was out of sight off I'd go. But at least I always beat the others when it came to questions on nature – leaves, nests and everythin' else. We used to be taken on nature walks.'

During his school-days Newton used to help his uncle with cleaning the kennels, heather burning and other keepering jobs, mostly on a Saturday morning. He left school at the customary age of fourteen. 'There was no advertisin' in them days – you were kind of 'anded down with jobs. Anyway, I 'ad the chance of two keeper positions – one at Bowes under Len Forester, and another at Malham Tarn, way over Masham country. But they meant I 'ad to leave home and you didn't like leavin' the dale, it was such a friendly place. Mind you, every man that's left has done very good, becoming policemen, keepers, etc, because I think the gentlemen knew we were all honest and trustworthy. And bein' a Hutchinson I was never refused a job.

'So I stayed at 'ome and did a bit of haytiming, rabbit catchin' etc – anythin' to get a bob or two. The farmers paid me about £1 a week for the rabbits, which I caught with snares and ferrets – boltin' and shootin' 'em. The rabbits was sold at Richmond. It was the farmer's wife's livin' then, 3d a couple for shot rabbits and 6d a couple for snared.

'But I did all sorts, includin' burnin' timber for one chap at Marske. And I was always out on shoots – the keepers really took to me. They knew I could take round a dozen beaters and know just where to put them. I suppose it was a sort of gift. But you could never get grouse beaters then unless all the farmers had already got their haytime in.

'We were always getting' together to shoot the foxes in the dale. The horses couldn't hunt there. It were that rocky they'd 'ave killed theirselves. I 'elped the keepers with this and we all got on together. Now where there's one keeper there used to be six.'

Newton was 'about twenty-three' before he took his first full-time keeping job. 'We were havin' bait [lunch] by a wall. There would 'ave been the usual mincemeat and taties in pastry, a cold bottle of tea (no flasks then man!), and perhaps a bit of cake or gooseberry pie. Then the headkeeper of Marske says to me, "When you gettin' married, Newton? I want an underkeeper." So I said, "I'll 'ave a go at both".

'So off I went to Marske, halfway between Reeth and Richmond, where my wages was three shillings short of £2. I 'ad a suit and a free house, but if you wanted wood you 'ad to get it yourself. The suit was "nigger" brown. The headkeeper gave us the cloth in a roll and you could 'ave any tailor you wanted. We was allowed £5 to make it up and I had Mr Clay from Leeds. He used to travel all round the farms and was a very good tailor. We 'ad a cap too, but I was always bein' pulled up for not wearin' mine. I had lovely curly hair in them days.'

At Marske, Newton's headkeeper was Milton Beattie from Northumberland, 'a grand feller. There were two of us under-keepers and a pheasant lad. The boss was Mr Martineau, who rented the shoot from D'arcy Hutton.

'We worked on both grouse and pheasants, and the rearin' was all broodies then. We used to buy the hen cluckers for 18d each if they sat, and if they didn't we very soon took 'em back. When they was finished we sold 'em for 3/6d to anyone as they'd lay their heads off.

'The boss used to come for six weeks. He was an American millionaire. But it was her [Mrs Martineau] that 'ad the money. She was a little devil.

'One day the head said to me, "When you go up to check your butts over take your gun and shoot a grouse". So I did, and put it in me pocket on shoot day as instructed. Meanwhile, the head met the boss by the hall to see how the wind was, to choose the beats. He always went by the weathercock.

'Away we went on my patch and eventually Mrs Martineau says to me, "There's a grouse down over there Hutchinson". But the boss said there wasn't. Anyway, I had to go with her to look for it. Then the headkeeper signalled me with his whistle and when she wasn't looking I dropped the grouse I 'ad in my pocket. After a bit she said, "Look Hutchinson, here it is". So I sent Silk for it and he retrieved to me before she could touch it.

'We took the grouse back to the boss, but he knew what was

goin' on. He felt the bird and whispered to me, "Look Hutchinson, it's cold. Never mind, you've put her in good tune" – yummer that is. And after that I couldn't do a thing wrong. You had to be cute then – tricks of the trade, boy.'

But it was certainly a hard life at Marske. 'From the 12th of August you 'ad to be up at 5am and over there, on parade – all black boots and done up – for the off at 9am. I often had to walk two miles four times a day on the pheasants and it was six miles to get to your moor. It was all shoemucker's gallowa' [shanks's pony] then. And every fourth day I 'ad to sit up all night watching, no matter if I were tired from the day before. Nowadays these keepers don't know they're born. It's the Land-Rovers that's spoiled it. In the old days you was out all day with your bottle of tea and you'd often walk miles before you even saw the heather.

'We had all black labradors then and all the good dogs were mine. It was nothin' for someone to pay £100 for a good animal then. They were good guard dogs too. When the pheasant lad was sent to fetch the baits [lunches] he could never get mine. My dog wouldn't let 'im anywhere near it!

'After a while the boss said we all 'ad to wear plus-fours, but I said to the others, "To hell with that, we've always 'ad breeches". Anyway, in the end we 'ad to 'ave them, and when I put them on, my wife, who used to knit my stockings, said I looked a fool. But my neighbour said to me, "Newton, you do look grand". Well, I was turning round in 'em and I thought someone was followin' me, they was so wide. Then I went over to the hall in 'em and one of the valets came over to me and said, "Good morning Mr Beattie". Then he realised who it was and said, "Good God, it's Hutchinson: you do look grand". That was in 1938, and from then on I wore plus-fours to the day I retired from full-time keeperin' in 1979.'

It was at Marske that Newton encountered the finest Shot he

has ever seen. 'We 'ad lots of grouse there but nobody could 'it 'em much, so one day Beattie said to Martineau, "I wish you'd get some better Shots in". Anyway, this 12th of August the wind was just right for my beat. After a bit Beattie says to me, "There's a man down there gone wild. I know I used to moan nobody could 'it anythin', but after 'im there won't be a grouse left on the place". Turned out it was Guy Moreton.

'Next day we 'ad to go over to Reeth moor to help and the same team of Guns was there. The poor ol' head up there – Jack Alderson – was cryin' they shot so many. My God, Guy Moreton didn't 'alf belt some grouse down. It was all double guns then. They 'ad colossal bags.'

In 1939 Newton was visited by 'an old brigadier who used to shoot with us. He said, "You'll be for the call up soon. You want to go and join the Royal Ordnance." So off I went to Leadenhall Street, Darlington, It was the first time I'd been to the town.

'At Darlington I wanted a smoke so badly I went into this shop with a Capstan sign and asked this lass if she could spare a packet of fags. Then two little kiddies came out and said, "Eh, it's the gamekeeper from Marske". They remembered me from when I let them go down to the waterfall. So after that their mum let me 'ave *twenty* Capstan, not just ten.

'When I arrived at Leadenhall Street there was keeper John Lambert from Coverdale there too. He'd been on the beer and when he 'ad to pee in the glass 'e filled it up so full it splashed all over when the doctor picked it up. Then 'e was passed grade two because 'e 'ad great big flat feet.

'After that a lad said to Lambert, "By gum, you've got a hairy chest", so Lambert thumped 'im right in the chest and 'e went flyin'. Then, when I was bein' sworn in, this specialist came rushin' out and said, "Stop, there's been a mistake". I was passed unmedically fit [unfit] for all forces because I'd had rheumatic fever as a lad. When I 'ad it I was wrapped up with cotton wool all around me to sweat it out. Mother looked after me and there was no penicillin in them days.'

Newton gratefully returned home to Marske, later discovering that the crafty brigadier had only recommended the Royal Ordnance because he was already in it and wanted the keeper he knew well to be his batman!

'In those days Beattie used to go to Grinton pub, near Reeth. When he was drunk he rode 'is motorbike fine, but as soon as 'e got off 'e fell flat on 'is back. At night you could see 'is light snakin' up those big 'ills. Anyway, one night I was ridin' pillion and when we got to the top of the hill I heard boom boom. So I said, "There's sumat goin' on, we'd better stop, what with the light an' all". "Bugger it", he said, "we'll press on." So we did, and on the Monday we 'eard that some bombs 'ad been dropped right on our moor – Copperthwaite, near Marrick.

'Poor old Beattie couldn't smell foxes or hear properly, you know. He was a gunner in the first war and suffered a terrible shock which left 'im like it.

'Another time at Marske, one sunny day in June, I 'eard this *pip pip pip* on Skelton moor and looked up to see a Spitfire after a German plane, which came down on Barnard Castle.

'Then there was a day when the air raid warden was blowin' 'is whistle all over the place and there was a big fire on the moor. I met Walter Lee – the Barningham keeper – and we ran up the valley together to see what was goin' on. Suddenly this great big airplane engine came rushin' down through a stone wall right by us. Further up we found two Germans on the ground still in their seats, all bloody and their legs smashed up. The rest of the plane was all over the place – there'd be bits there yet. And I bet the wall's still down where the engine just missed us. There were one or two sheep killed too.'

During the war Newton volunteered as a special constable at Richmond. 'It was a good job. They sent me round all the gentlemen's houses to make sure all their lights were out. Some of 'em were shootin' men I already knew and they used to look after me. One feller used to leave a bottle of beer out for me every night.

'Bein' a special helped me enormous with the poachin'. The local inspector used to put all the newly-wed police on duty at Marske and tell 'em, "You've got some good friends there – that's the keepers". And if they put a foot wrong he'd send 'em off to Catterick Camp or some other place where there was some real thievin'.'

Eventually, 'Marske was sold and the farmers bought their farms when the Martineau lease was up. Sir James Baird of Middleton Lodge took the shooting. Only the headkeeper was kept on and it was arranged for me to replace Beattie when he retired. But they didn't sack me. D'arcy Hutton was very good to me and said that I was not to be thrown out of my house.'

However, without any regular income, Newton was forced to look for a job. 'I opened the *Stockton and Darlington Times* on the Saturday and saw, "Wanted – gamekeeper – Barnard Castle district. Apply A. W. Watts, Northallerton." He was Major Morrit's agent for Rokeby.

'On the Sunday I told Beattie about it and on the Monday 'e took me on 'is motorbike to see our agent, Benjamin Taylor of Leyburn. Taylor just picked up the phone and arranged for me to meet A. W. Watts at the Morrit Arms.

'I went to the interview by bus, all expenses paid. When I arrived there was half a dozen of us picked out, all walkin' up and down in front of the pub, not much said. Then I was recognised and one of the others said, "Oh no, it's a Hutchinson; he'll get the job – we might as well go home".

'When I saw the agent 'e said, "By God, you're a big feller". I said, "I'm not to cross". Then we soon got down to brass tacks – house, money etc. So I started there in 1940, for about the same wages as before, just the headkeeper and me, apart from when his son joined us later.'

But things did not always go smoothly at Rokeby. 'Once the major 'ad some guests over on leave and 'e decided 'e would let them shoot on the Sunday as the game laws was changed specially for the war. Well, it was the only time in my life I've shot on a Sunday and I didn't like it one bit. Sunday was Sunday. To ask a man to turn out after he'd done six days a week – well! Still, it didn't 'appen again.'

Bags at Rokeby were about 100 – all pheasants. 'We managed to do a bit of feedin' durin' the war as we gave the farmers a day's rabbitin' and they gave us the rakin's off the fields.'

Although Newton was at Rokeby for eight years, he did not really like it there. 'People used to say, "How's that keeper got out the war?" I always said we should 'ave 'ad badges sayin' medically unfit for service.

'We 'ad a lot of poachers from Barnard Castle too. They always said they was pickin' mushrooms but they was really settin' snares for rabbits. Mind you, we 'ad a few at Marske as well. But it's all part of the game. There was a clique at Richmond did it for the money and you 'ad one or two scraps. But in those days we were police on the land, you know. The real police couldn't even come on the estate without your say so.

'I've never been injured by poachers. I've always waded in first. If I struck at someone runnin' away it was always at their ankles. Then they dropped like a rabbit.'

Not surprisingly, some of Newton's assailants would end up needing medical attention. 'But my old doctor – Williams at Richmond – never 'ad much sympathy for 'em as they was in

the wrong. He was a shootin' man and never sent me a bill –
even when my boy 'ad pneumonia. He always said 'e 'd take it
out of someone who 'ad money.'

In 1948 Newton was told, 'to go for a single-handed keeper's
job at Clervaux Castle, Croft, near Darlington. I was there for
four years, for C. W. D. Chater, solicitor. It was poached to
death. I caught about six or eight a week and got it squared up
like, but you were never done. It was all pheasants, partridges
and duck, and I didn't like it there.

'Then one day this police sergeant came to the lodge. He said,
"I've been lookin' for you for years". He'd been keeper boy long
before me back at Rokeby and 'e 'eard they wanted a keeper at
Raby. The police sergeant there 'ad been askin' around and
Hanson said I was highly recommended.

'They wanted me in the cabin at Raby, but I didn't like it and
turned it down. So they asked me to Selaby. That was poached
and trespassed to death, but I took it and it was the best place I
ever 'ad. I went there in 1954 and for the first time ever I 'ad a
bathroom and runnin' water out of a tap. There was even fire
logs – everythin' I wanted. It suited me fine and I stayed there
till I retired, twenty-six years later. Back in the dale the water
ran off the hill into a stone trough 100yds from the house and
you 'ad to take a bucket and cup to it.'

Putting up with relatively primitive domestic conditions was
all the more remarkable when you consider the hard winters
which high-ground keepers and their families have often had to
endure. The worst that Newton can recall was that of 1946–7,
when he was at Rokeby. 'Cut off? Good God man! My wife and
children nearly starved. When it was over I think we just finished with only a chair and table in the house. We 'ad to use
everythin' we 'ad to keep warm. It took me half a day rather
than half an hour to get down to Barnard Castle. When I got

there I bought a three-gill bottle of paraffin and a bit of flour and yeast – that was about all I could carry. There was a hell of a lot of dead sheep on the moor.

'There was a bad time in early '63 too. After a good breedin' season there was a lot of wild English partridges at Selaby, so we brought some of 'em into the hall and Lady Barnard was tryin' to warm 'em up and dry 'em out by the fire.'

'People often say to me, "How did you get the job at Raby?" and I always say, "Good manners". In the old days if I was comin' up the lane and saw someone pass me who was older than me I had to raise my cap. That's how it was then. You always showed respect.' Indeed, I am reliably informed by Newton's son, Brian, that hat protocol was so ingrained in his father's character he even put his cap on to answer the telephone for the first six months after it was installed!

But for all his good manners, Newton insists that he, 'never got a tip till I came to Raby, where I became second keeper.' Even then he was generally more impressed by people's integrity and skill than their money. One of the great highlights of his life was when he shook hands with Prince Charles, who came to hunt locally. 'Lord Barnard said to me a while later, "I hear you've met Prince Charles". I said, "Yes milord, and I've not washed my hand since, though it were a month ago".'

However, not all celebrities have created the right impression. 'When I was loading at Lowther I met Charlie Drake, the comedian, who was shootin'. He 'ad two silly pheasant tail feathers in his hat and was squeakin' all over the place. In the end he was shoutin' so much and spoilin' the drives the head told him to shut up.'

In pest control Newton was always a great believer in traps. 'They was catchin' 'em while you were sleepin'.' His favourite was the 'Samson', a simple, home-made, dead-fall device in which the victim dislodges a baited wooden-peg support and is trapped under a stone slab. 'See all these slabs in the yard. There's one there for every size up to cat, and they've all caught well.'

Despite his praise of the past, Newton has not been against all modern inventions. After years of walking everywhere he was certainly glad to get some motorised transport of his own. 'I 'ad a motorbike first, a Norman 2-stroke which cost £21. People could 'ear me comin' for miles around and I passed me test on it. After that I 'ad a brand-new BSA 250. Then I bought a BSA 600. By hell, that could move and I caught many a poacher on that. But as I got older I got a bit cold on the bike so I bought a Robin Reliant three-wheeler, which I 'ad for twenty-one years.

'At Marske all the keepers that came along for a job could shoot OK, but when the head sent 'em to me to check, they hadn't got a clue when settin' a trap. You've got to camouflage to make it natural. And I used to spend a lot of time studyin' the vermin, mister. You watch for all the signs. Listen to that blackbird – *plop plop plop* – he's tellin' you somethin's there.'

Today Newton still takes a close interest in the wildlife around his home on The Green, at Piercebridge. He retired to the yellow-washed cottage, which bears the Barnard estate crest, in 1979. But with blood circulation problems now he rarely travels far, preferring to sit outside, enjoying the magnificent garden now tended by son Brian, or reflecting on old times at the splendid George Inn, where Dick Turpin is said to have hidden. Indeed, he has become almost a landmark within the village, one who always keeps an eye on things. 'If anybody goes away here they always come and tell me.'

Newton did not plunge into full retirement. Indeed, the estate asked him to become head gardener when he left the moor. 'I didn't know one flower from another, but I went. And I wouldn't start till 8.30am – I was sick of this 6 o'clock in the mornin' stuff. It was a big garden of ten acres and I was in charge of three others, but I didn't 'ave any real work to do. I only did it for a few months.

'After that the curator of the castle asked me to go on the gate taking the tickets. But I said, "You've got the wrong feller. I'm the one who shifts 'em out, not gets 'em in.".'

Since then Newton has taken things at a much more leisurely pace. His wife Joyce died some years ago and he now lives alone, but he sees a lot of his son Brian and his four daughters. He also remains at the centre of the shooting grapevine.

Newton Hutchinson has clearly enjoyed his career, especially his time at Raby, where he has been very well looked after. 'My pay was never a ha'penny wrong. If I were a 14-year-old I'd do it all again.' And even now, given half a chance, I believe the man sitting quietly, puffing his pipe, would seize the opportunity to relive some of the old times. After all, his wardrobe still contains some of his heavy-tweed keeper's suits going back several decades. It's as if he is expecting to be called back into service at any moment.

A MATCH FOR ANY POACHER

———— ⚬⚬⚬⚬⚬ ————

Any poacher who dared tackle George Cole in his prime inevitably came off worse because this renowned keeper was also an expert boxer. Indeed, in 1936 he was the sparring partner of Tommy Farr when the British champion fought Max Baer for the world title. This came about because both men trained at the Green Man on Blackheath. 'And 'e was bloody rough with his sparring partners too. But the first time I had a go I was still on me feet after three rounds. So we did the same the next day and after that I was given complimentary tickets for the big fight.'

At that time George was in the Metropolitan Police, but not surprisingly he 'could not stand being shut up in the town' and it was not long before he felt the need to get back into the keeping life, which was such a strong tradition in his family.

One of only two children, George Cole was born on 10 March 1916, at his maternal grandparents' house at Cookham in Berkshire, his father being away in the war. His paternal grandfather was headkeeper for thirty years up to retirement at the nearby Penn estate, where he headed a team of fourteen underkeepers, including George's father and three uncles. They wore bowler hats and velvet livery with brass buttons.

The first thing George can remember is, 'rolling around in grandad's churn. He kept dog biscuits in it and I was well and truly stuck so auntie had to get me out. Grandad had two kennels – one for flat-coats and another for curly-coated retrievers. I never liked the curlies as they bit.

'Grandad fed the pheasants at Penn on a sort of stiff custard made from eggs and milk. The birds apparently thrived on it – and I should think the keepers had to let their suits out a bit at the end of the season.

'I also remember seeing newts in the well-water when we raised the lid, so that shows how fresh it was.'

When George was three the family moved to Ambergate, in Derbyshire, where his father was underkeeper on the Belper estate. And when he was seven they moved to the Foremark estate [now Repton School], Derbyshire, where father became headkeeper.

'From Foremark I had about four miles to walk to school at Ticknall, but I didn't mind. On the way there I used to trap moles and skinned 'em as I went. I got a tanner [2½p] apiece for 'em. The estate also had a full-time mole catcher who worked for a farthing an acre.

'I liked school and even went to evening classes. I never missed – and we often had four-foot snowdrifts. It was always cold up there, but coal was cheap as we weren't far from the mines. The food was good too. But although I liked lessons I never saw any farther then goin' into keepering.'

George left school at the age of fourteen and went to work in the gardens at Sir Francis Burdett's Foremark Hall, knowing that a keepering vacancy was coming up. 'I was keeperin' for father anyway.

'In the garden I earned 7/6d a week. There were half a dozen of us, with three or four living in a bothy. There was a tremendous amount of mowing, but not for me – I just wheeled barrow loads of grass away. It seemed to be cold all the time there – except when you were digging.

'When I was fifteen I became keeper's boy, doin' anythin' that nobody else wanted to do. I got ten bob a week, of which I was allowed to keep half-a-crown. It was an enjoyable time. There was a lot more happiness in the countryside in those days and the communities stayed in the villages.

'One year, millions of starlings came into our larch plantation, where I had six- to seven-week-old pheasants. They ruined the wood with their droppings and breaking the branches, and there was a 2- to 3-inch runnin' mass underneath. We tried every way to shift 'em – hawk kites, sulphur fires and shooting – but it did no good and we had to abandon the wood. The birds eventually left in the spring and millions of elder trees came up under the roost, from the seeds in the berries they'd been eating.

'I had my first night-poaching case when I was seventeen. It was seven in the evening and I was just settin' the alarm guns around the woods – you never set 'em early as the pheasants would trigger 'em going to roost – when three or four shots went off. I ran round to cut the culprits off and met two blokes with some pheasants and a .410. Then we had a bit of a set to and one man bent the gun barrel over me head. But I had this ash plant with a ferrule on the end and I hit him on the head with it, splitting the stick and my hand too. I had a go at the other one as well but in the end we had to give up and off they went.

'I had an idea who the men were and biked four miles to fetch the village policeman. When we went round one was at home but he denied it. However, the police found the .410 in his lavatory. They got the other man the next day. I went with the police to where he was working on a road gang, and when we lifted his cap there was the bloody great gash I gave him. Both men got two years inside.

'After the war I was playin' darts at a pub in Repton when I saw this chap and he took his cap off and said, "Just run your hand over this". It was the poacher I hit all that time ago and he still had a ridge in his skull to prove it.

'When I was nineteen, Major Betterton – the shoot leader – urged me to join the police, saying there was no future in keeping. So I did. But you had to be twenty to join the county force and I couldn't wait, so I went to the Metropolitan, who took you younger.

'I did a bit of everything. I was on the beat and out in the old Wolseley 25s – there were only a few cars then – and had a turn in the CID. Also I had to do a month's traffic duty in the Blackwall tunnel, but it was much quieter in those days. The only trouble was the trams – they wouldn't stop for anybody because they were frightened they'd get stuck on the dead patch.

'There was nothing too vicious then: most people were satisfied with a decent punch-up. Just pop 'em in the old Black Maria and off to Blackheath. There was no real malice in those days. Anyone we run in we'd probably have a drink with the next night.'

After three years George longed for the green fields again and in 1938 went along to Cruft's. 'It was good then because you really felt at home there. Anyway, I met Dickinson – the head-keeper at Somerley, near Ringwood in Hampshire, and was taken on as second keeper on the spot. There were five keepers at Lord Normanton's estate then.'

Somerley has long been renowned for the variety of wildfowl which visit the river there, as well as its pheasants. The duck have been shot using the old system of gazes [blinds] which enable the Guns to approach the river unseen. 'There were several miles of these along the river and two old pensioners spent the whole of every summer making them. They scythed the spear grass and threaded it between rails. It was a work of art. After the war there was not so much spear grass so I added birch.

'On a duck shoot I stood where all the Guns could see me drop a flag and start walking in together, so that everyone had a fair chance. We only shot it three or four times a year. In those days even the farm workers were not allowed to walk the meadows in case the duck were disturbed. A punt was used to pick up the shot birds, and that took some doing in a current of three of four knots. One old chap was so strong he always had dry elbows at the end of it. The bag was just under 500 a day in 1947. We also used to get lots of snipe and once killed seventy in an hour.'

Wildfowl shooting had always been George's favourite form of the sport. 'I've only ever shot one partridge in my life. I always thought it far too nice a bird. Whenever they wanted a brace or two for the house I used to send old Jack.'

In 1939, the year before he married Marjorie at Repton, George joined the 26th Light Ack-ack Regiment at Tutbury, in Derbyshire. 'We never had a uniform – just walked about in an old rugby scarf and greatcoat and went rabbitin' in between going' round the country. I was never much of a military chap – never liked polishin' stones.

'The best bit was when we were stationed at Hatfield. I aways carried my 16-bore with me in the kitbag in case of a bit of a shoot. I often used to get hares, pheasants and wildfowl – with the permission of the farmers. After a while Captain Grierson heard about it and he wanted to join in too. He wasn't a military chap either. We were only part-time soldiers. Sometimes we got rabbits and all sorts of game and used to swap it.'

After further postings abroad, George left the Army in 1946, obviously without much regard for the medals he acquired. He turned the campaign stars into keyrings, which he still uses. 'They gave a nasty jab in the leg so there's not much chance of losing them.'

He did not intend to go back into keeping after the war. 'I thought it was too hard and I'd got used to having my nights off.'

So he became a country and land drainage officer, 'in charge of the prisoners as I could speak their language a bit. But we could not get the Italians to work, so I decided to put a Jerry in charge of 'em as the Germans were so efficient. That soon stopped 'em going 'round the shops and after the girls.'

Later that year George returned to Somerley, to work on the river for two years before becoming headkeeper. 'When I went back the gyppos had taken charge. The first lot I came across was two pickin' daffodils by the house, so I went straight up and challenged them – I was really fit then. I smacked the tall one straight in the midriff and he fell about 12ft onto the concrete support of the bridge. Then the little one ran off. I was really worried about the chap who'd fallen, but up 'e got and off he went.

'Anyway, I thought I'd better go to see his lordship and tell him all about it in case anything came of it. I thought he might rollick me for being too rough, but instead he said, "Good – I'll pay the fine if there is one and you sort the rest of them out". So after that we really gave the gyppos a tough time.'

At that time the estate also suffered through a large number of otters going into the trout hatchery. 'It was easy meat for them', George remembers. 'So I had six Lane's double-spring, 6in spiked-jaw otter traps made. The ordinary gins wouldn't hold the otter. I always remember old man Lane – he had a gold Albert across his chest and a little gold trap attached to it.

'One year we caught thirty-odd otters, but now I regret it. No one then would have dreamed that the otter would become so rare. Trapping them was perfectly legal then. The best one weighed over 30lb and their skins were worth £3 10s each.

'It was about that time the landlord of the Fish Inn – Johnny Frampton – used to come picking-up regularly. One day a hen pheasant got up and was wounded. Obviously we didn't want it to get away and were so insistent that a Gun shot at it dangerously before it disappeared into a withy bed. Unfortunately, although Johnny hid his head round a stack he forgot how much his stomach stuck out, so he got peppered in the gut.

'Luckily Johnny wasn't badly hurt and this gave George the opportunity for a little fun, through making an unusual entry on the game card. As usual, Lord Normanton read out the bag at dinner that evening: "… pheasants and one Frampton. What's a Frampton?" Of course, this brought tremendous laughter, but George had warned Colonel Wright, one of the Guns, about the prank, so it was taken in the right spirit.

'That morning Johnny Frampton had also backed the horse Tent Peg, and won £100, so he ended up with gold and lead on the same day.' Johnny was obviously delighted with the way things turned out and gave George an old bottle of whisky to commemorate the occasion. That treasured bottle still remains unopened in the Cole household.

On another occasion at Somerley it was George who was on the receiving end of a shot. 'I was out rabbitin' with old Jack Reed – a wartime keeper, when he accidentally peppered me from only five yards. Luckily I had a leather jacket on, but it was shredded and I had eighteen pellets in me back. I went to see the family doctor and he said, "Well, I'll squeeze a few out, but we'll never get the rest". So he did and off I went to the Fish. A few noggins cure most things. I always reckon the drink must have come out the holes in me back and cauterised 'em. Poor old Jack Reed was there, drowning his sorrows, but he'd thrown his gun away and said he'd never shoot again.'

In the early 1960s George found a mink's nest in a rabbit hole in a wood called the Dog Kennels. 'The authorities didn't believe it at first as it was one of the first in the country, and the story was on TV. The farm it escaped from offered £1 each animal, so I thought why bother – I might as well skin them myself. So I ended up selling them to the Hudson Bay Company, through London. When they were cured, matched up and auctioned they fetched a really good price – £12 to £18 a skin. This went to two of the four underkeepers who picked 'em up in catch-'em-alive traps.'

George obviously had great affection for the late Lord Normanton – the fifth Earl. 'He often used to ring up for me just to go and have a chat in the kitchen. He had such a fund of wonderful stories and he was a good friend. One day I came across him by the river. I'd heard this *tick tick tick* and wondered what it was. He was sitting there peacefully with his feet in the water and his bike upside down, turning the pedals by hand. I said, "What's to do m'lord?" and he said, "It's much easier to sit here doing this than that damn exercise my wife wants". Apparently, whenever he returned home, Lady Normanton would look at his mileometer to check that he had done the required twelve miles to get his weight down. He also used to sneak off to smoke – always had Trumper's Silk Cut – handmade for him.'

The fifth Earl died in 1967 and in 1973 George decided to take a job as headkeeper for Sir George Meyrick at Bodorgan, Anglesey. He retired there at the age of sixty-five and in the same year received his CLA forty-year service medal from Prince Charles at the Bowood Game Fair. He was succeeded as head by his son, Walter.

When George first went to Anglesey, 'old Jack Jones had keepered the estate for thirty years and said he'd never seen a fox! And they told me there were no foxes at all on Anglesey, but I shot one here within only a few weeks.

'At first I thought Anglesey were paradise – just like Somerley used to be, with hardly any traffic. But there were thousands and thousands of corvids and pigeons, and with all the crows and jackdaws sat round about every tree looked like it was covered with apples. So we set to work and cleared up all the rookeries. The trouble is a lot of farmers don't like to see 'em shot. There aren't many trees here – mostly only a few around the farmhouses, and the owners are superstitious enough to think that if the crows go the money goes too.'

Looking back on a very full life, George told me, 'I couldn't have picked a nicer set of employers.' In serving them he has certainly met a few characters and celebrities and has witnessed some fine sport. 'Lord Eldon was the best Shot I ever saw. Raoul Millais – the artist – could really shoot too.'

But others were not always to be admired. 'There was old 110% Cobbold, the banker, who lined birds up before shooting. And Peter Playdel-Bouverie always shot two Guns' width either side of him: if he was in the middle of the line the whole lot would be in jeopardy. The boss always used to say, "Oh no!" if he drew the peg next to him.'

While at Somerley, George was a frequent visitor to nearby Broadlands, where his son Walter was second keeper to the famous Harry Grass. 'We didn't even dare tell Dad that the Queen was coming', Walter told me. 'Anyway, he was picking up in Town Copse and at the end of it a woman shouted across, "I think we've finished here", so Dad called back, "OK, we'll amble on up now". Imagine his surprise when he discovered it was the Queen.'

George was also picking up at Broadlands on the record day when Prince Philip laid his guns down on the grass because the barrels were too hot. 'He shot 200 at one stand alone. In fact he, Lord Brabourne and Cunningham-Reid had 200 each at Town Copse. They shot 2,000 that day and in the evening I said to Grass I wouldn't like to open Lord Louis' post next morning when the antis get to hear about it. Well, Harry went and told this to his boss and afterwards he sent back the message, "Tell Cole he's bloody well right".

THEIR MAJESTIES' KEEPER

———— ∞∞∞ ————

When Jack Clark marched behind the coffin of George VI along with the other Sandringham keepers there were tears in his eyes, for he had seen the passing not only of a great Shot but also of a man devoted to shooting and all its followers. Jack's father was also in that procession from Sandringham Church to Wolferton Station in 1952, marking a long family commitment to the royal family.

'George VI really liked duck shooting and rabbit shooting best', Jack told me at his very attractive Victorian retirement cottage at West Newton on the Sandringham estate. 'We often had to walk the woods for him in between main shooting days, so we was never done. But he had to slacken up in the last few years when he became ill.

'I spoke to him on the hare shoot the day before he died: he said goodnight to us and we said goodnight to him. Everything seemed much the same as usual.

'Next day we was pushin' a load of rabbits home on a bike when we met the farm foreman. He said "I suppose you know the news". "No," we all chirruped together. And with a lump in his throat he said "The King's dead. Old Jimmy McDonald the valet found him when he took up his cup of tea".'

Christened John, Jack Clark was born on 29 April 1923 at Great Wilbraham, Cambridgeshire, where his father and his grandfather before him had been keeper for Squire Hicks.

In 1934 the family moved to Sandringham, when Jack's father, Nobby, became beat keeper at Flitcham. And after schooling, fourteen-year-old Jack not surprisingly started work in 1937 on the Wolferton beat, where he was to remain for the whole of his working life, apart from war service. 'In those days there were very few job opportunities so you took what you could. I might have gone in the Army, but you had to take a test and I weren't too good at arithmetic.' For a month or two before starting on pheasant work Jack worked as houseboy for the retired schoolmaster who looked after the King's racing pigeons. 'When the old boy died the lofts were closed.'

Working under his father, Jack did a lot of vermin trapping and, as 'the junior', he was heavily involved in the routine feeding programme which included the usual mix of eggs, rice, scalded biscuit meal and 'hundreds and hundreds of minced, boiled rabbits. We fed three or four times a day and the food stove never went out, even if it was pissin' with rain.

'All the coops were kept in a great big shed and for days on end we had to scrub them out with Jeyes Fluid, and then they were limewashed. And all the runs had to be creosoted.

'Each clutch was made up to about twenty eggs and it was very important that the broods were kept separated. So we put each chick in a little marked bag to make sure they all ended up with the right hens after being crated to the rearing field about a mile away – the hens would brain the wrong chicks.

'Each coop contained a faggot of rhododendron for the chicks to hide in till the grass got high, and we moved the coops every day. The chicks demanded a great deal of attention so we used to pray for a cold night so that we could shut them up early and not have to watch them.

'Days were specially long if there was big vermin trouble and we sometimes had to stay in the cabins all night. And you know what it's like working for father. Not only did he make me gather all the firewood in a pony and cart, but I had to take him his dinner on me bike, too!

'We were on the rearing field for six to eight weeks as there were two hatches. When the first lot went to wood it was often two weeks before the others would be off. One of our biggest problems was that if they was sick there were no drugs to dose the birds up: all we could do was shift 'em to fresh ground and hope they would get better.'

With the outbreak of war almost all rearing stopped at Sandringham. Jack joined the Army at the end of 1941 and returned home in 1946. Shooting had continued at Sandringham during the war, when there were some good partridge years – about 6,000 were shot one season. 'With the letdown of the war, wild pheasants and partridges found ideal conditions here and really came into their own. There was no going back to the old days of heavy rearing, when they thought nothing of shooting 2,000 pheasants or 300–400 brace of partridges on a single outing. The total number shot must have been enormous and we always wondered how accurate the gamebooks were. Large quantities were sent off to market and somebody must have made a fortune.

'In those days neighbouring estates too were taken for the shooting, but that all finished with Edward VIII. On some beats, if they didn't kill more than 2,000 the first time over then someone was for the high jump.

'Father had a lighter suit for partridge shooting, which often took place in fine weather early in the season, but for pheasant days he wore a big, dark-green beatkeeper's coat, cord breeches, gaiters and a hard bowler hat with gold braid sash and two acorns around. It was ever such a heavy coat – what it would cost today goodness only knows.'

Before the war the beaters wore blue, numbered smocks, 'and there were two gangs of them on partridge days as there was no transport to whizz people around in. In fact there were still two gangs for a while after the war.'

In those days the keeper's lunch consisted of 'a great chunk of bread – about half a cottage loaf, cheese, meat, beer and mince pies – all wrapped up in a little parcel. The Guns had a special marquee for lunch, and headkeeper Bland had his own little tent adjoining it. Mother did out our big front room for the loaders of the guests, but we used to be all right for grub for about a fortnight afterwards, what with sauces, cold meats, pickles, chutneys and suchlike.

'Headkeeper Bland was not a popular man. He looked just like George V and rode about on a pony checking up on everybody. All the keepers had to call him "Sir" – you wouldn't have dared address him by his Christian name in those days.'

At first Jack earned 'Ten or twelve bob a week', but after paying his keep ended up with 'only about two bob pocket money', so he was much better off in the Army, when he had the whole of his ten bob pay to spend.

No doubt his Army experience helped prepare him for the inevitable occasional brush with poachers. Jack's worst experience was in 1955, when he came across a gang of three at night. 'I fetched one bloke down but the other buggers came back at me. I was on the ground when I saw the raised gun and instinctively put my hand up to defend myself. I'm sure that saved me from having a clobbered skull, but the rifle butt did smash several ribs.

'But I had my own back once or twice. Father did too. Take the time when he struggled with a man holding a .410 and the gun went off right next to his head when he was holding it by the muzzle. The man got away, but next day they found the gun's fore-end along with a box of matches at the scene of the incident.

'The following Sunday a gang of five from Wisbech were seen poaching on another part of the estate and were picked up by the police. Next morning the police inspector found that one of the gang's guns matched the fore-end found the week before. The police knew one of the gang well – a seventeen-year-old – so put the heat on him and he coughed the lot. Just before the war that was.'

A bachelor most of his life, Jack married in 1980 – quite a change for the man who, prior to retirement in April 1988, lived for fifty years in the same cottage in Wolferton woods.

When I visited him at his pretty little estate house, he told me: 'The Duke of Edinburgh and Prince Charles are excellent Shots, though Charles doesn't do much shooting now and Philip gets bad arthritis in his hands: you always know when it's playing him up on a cold day because he misses more than usual and then swears a lot. Lord Brabourne is perhaps the best Shot I've seen, though he can be a bit greedy. Prince Edward is not a particularly good Shot. The Queen never shoots, but what a keen gundog lady she is. All the dogs love her and make a great fuss of her. She had handled my old bitch Pendle and now whenever the dog sees Her Majesty she will make straight for her – even if she is a hundred yards away. All she wants is a bit of fuss made of her.

'Overall, it's been a good life, but I've certainly had some hassle. I'm the sort of bloke who worries and would have been no good as a headkeeper. I don't know if I'd do it all over again. I missed the Army you know, especially when I was demobbed. When you came back to a little ol' bloody village like Wolferton after years abroad nobody knew you, and you couldn't join up with the regulars if you were all crocked up like I was with my injuries.'

Jack died in July 1997.

THE WORLD'S OLDEST KEEPER?

————— ◦◦◦◦◦ —————

When 24-year-old George Pryke had 'a dose of gas' on the Somme towards the end of World War I, he never in his wildest dreams imagined that he would be fit enough to continue full-time keepering into his one hundreth year. Yet he did just that, with great distinction, despite having his hearing permanently damaged by shell-fire and experiencing increasingly frequent dizzy spells.

Born on 18 December 1893, at Condover, in Shropshire, George left school at the age of fourteen, and did 'a bit of rabbiting and post work – deliveries and so on' before starting under his gamekeeper father at Dudmaston at the age of fifteen. There, three keepers reared just six or seven hundred pheasants, although most of George's work was on the main partridge beat.

With a good stock of wild birds to look after, his main task was to keep the vermin down. 'There were lots of stoats about – I trapped thirty-five in my first week, in 1908, with the ordinary steel gin. I was paid about nine or ten bob a week; the head then had about a guinea a week and a farm worker 13s or 14s. But we also managed to nab a few cats and their skins were worth 4s each. A lot of farmers kept cats for killing rats and mice, but they didn't feed them of course, and they often got onto a partridge beat, where they did a lot of damage. Mind you, we had to be careful about killing them, and still sometimes got into trouble.'

In common with keepers on most other estates, George received one suit of clothes a year. 'Colonel Witmore used to go salmon fishing to Norway a great deal so he used to send wool over there to have cloth made up, and from this our local tailor made the suits.

'The beaters wore just ordinary clothes. Their pay was 2s 6d men and bob a day lads. There was no trouble getting beaters as long as you had plenty of beer – 7d a pint it was then, and it used to come out in big stone jars – three or four gallons each.'

In time-honoured fashion, George plotted all the partridge nests on a map of his beat, and understandably it was most dispiriting to see foxes making great inroads into his charges. 'It was all good hunting country so we weren't supposed to shoot the devils, but we all had ways of getting round this. We usually shot the adults and fed a few cubs, which the huntsman would see and go home happy. Yes, there were plenty of tricks in those days.'

Another of his wrinkles was to ring the nests with oil of tar or animal oil to stop dogs and foxes scenting the sitting partridges which 'had a lot of heat and scent in them.'

Considering all the trouble that keepers such as George took in caring for their birds, it was sometimes very disappointing to see a poor team of Guns let loose on them. For example, there was the day when the Johnson brothers (the tarmac people who rented part of the Dudmaston shooting) invited no less than fourteen business colleagues to shoot, and they were all inexperienced Guns. 'The shooting was fast and furious', said George, 'and one Gun gave me a bob to go and fetch his second cartridge bag, but it didn't do him or anyone else any good. On that drive they shot only seven and a half brace where they should have shot fifty. One Gun was honest enough to admit he didn't stand a chance, and gave me his gun to carry all day long.

'In those days none of the toffs was really liked – they were up there and you were down here' said George, raising and lowering his hand. 'But times have certainly changed for the better and now everyone mixes in together.

'The Guns used to go to one of the farms for lunch but the keepers and beaters always took their own. No one went home sober. The chauffeur was always sent to the local pub to refill the beaters' beer jars, and the Guns always had a crate of whisky – not just one bottle.'

At the end of August 1914, twenty-year-old George volunteered for the Shropshire Yeomanry. He became a despatch rider and carried many important messages on his motorbike, with strict instructions to deliver them only to a small number of specified people, irrespective of rank. First he went to Palestine, then France in 1918. 'The only compliment I ever got from an officer was "You bloody fool". I could have taken stripes in 1914, but I refused. I said I was looking after myself and no one else in this bloody war.'

When George returned from the war in January 1919 – fortunately in the first draft because he had a job to go to – he was very ill and weighed only 8st 4lb. But he soon picked up as he settled back into the routine of country life.

In 1923 he went to work for Colonel Walter Kynaston at Hardwick, near Ellesmere, Shropshire. The place was very run down, the old keeper had died and there was not a trap to be seen, though the land was hunted over.

Hardwick had been in the Kynaston family since 1730 and remained chiefly a partridge shoot till the great decline of the species after World War II.

George knew the present Colonel Kynaston (son of Walter) – 'Mr John' – since he was nine. 'I taught him to fish and shoot and he's quite a good Shot now.'

Not surprisingly after this long relationship, it was with some trepidation that 'Mr John' ordered the shoot's first ever poults in 1988, for until then George had reared pheasants using broody hens, the traditional method. But then this has never been a large shoot, and is still a purely family concern.

In earlier years George used to catch-up pheasants and later bought eggs to place under broodies. But in his final years he found 'hens hard to come by – in the old days they were just 2s 6d each, but do you know, in 1987 I had to pay £3 for one!' But you have to remember that George could recall when a good tip was 2s 6d and a £1 was something to talk about in the pub.

He also remembered when his favourite Gold Block tobacco was just 11d for a 2oz tin. Now it costs £2.94p 'but I only smoke 4oz a week. I've smoked since I was nine, and for many years it was fifty cigarettes a day before I changed to the pipe.

'But keepers were never what you would call poor. You could always shoot a rabbit and when I was a boy, for just half-a-crown you could buy a lump of meat big enough to feed a hungry family.'

Not surprisingly for an ex-despatch rider and a man who rode big motorbikes for most of his life, George's earliest memory concerned the roads. 'All they were was just rough Jew stones* rolled into sand. And you couldn't go anywhere without a puncture, if you were lucky enough to have tyres.'

But the man who devoted his life to sport – he could even remember shooting live pigeons from traps before it was outlawed – had no son to whom he could pass on his great store of knowledge. His wife Elizabeth died in 1969 after forty-three years of marriage, and in his final years his only companion was his dog Rumbo, 'given to me by Jimmy McAlpine, who used to shoot here a lot and named most of his dogs after drinks'.

Even in his nineties, George still had that special walk which distinguished the old partridge keeper, conscientiously stooping along every hedgerow, carefully marking and observing every nest. What a familiar sight he must have been in the pre-war patchwork-quilt countryside of Shropshire, and I wonder how many miles of tarred string he used to protect his partridge nests over so many years. Nor did he use any old bits of paper attached to the string: 'It had to be *The Field* as none of the other magazines or papers were strong enough!'

George died peacefully on 21 January, 1994, just one month after celebrating his 100th birthday, when he was still working as a full-time gamekeeper at Hardwick.

*A local name for hard, unmanageable rocks

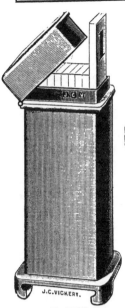

OVERCOMING TYRANNY

———— ∞∞∞ ————

Despite starting his career under one of the most tyrannical headkeepers this century, the late Charles South went on to become one of the most successful and respected exponents of his profession. When we met, Charlie remembered bitterly every detail of that cruel regime at Windsor Great Park in the Twenties.

Born 10 November 1908 at Rushton, Hertfordshire, Charlie grew up in a keepering family, but when he left school his father said he would be better off mole trapping and advised him to get six dozen traps to make a start. This he did, catching about forty moles a week and selling their skins for 5d each. In addition, he went beating with his father at Six Mile Bottom and on the celebrated neighbouring estates of Stetchworth and Dullingham for 7s a day and a pint of beer, 'but we had to take our own lunch'.

At the age of fifteen he became woodman for Six Mile Bottom at 26s a week, and continued in the post till he was nineteen, when his father took him to Crufts to get him a keepering job, the famous show acting as a sort of keepers' clearing house in the old days.

At Crufts Charlie met the headkeeper of Windsor Great Park, and thus began 'the worst year of my life. E. R. Dadley was to prove a real ogre. He was a right bugger and got me there under false pretences. I was supposed to be a keeper's help but spent all my time milking cows, sawing wood, gardening, looking after chickens and pigs, and even growing mangel-wurzels for the cattle – bloody slavery.'

His pay was 36s a week, but out of this he had to pay a guinea for his lodgings, and he was not given any special clothes. 'The proper keeper then had 37s 6d a week plus one suit of clothes a year.

'Just about the first words Dadley said to me were: "No drinking and no smoking, and if I ever catch you off the estate you'll get a minute's notice." We even had to ask permission to get a haircut, and when this was given we had to be back in double-quick time.'

At Windsor Charlie was one of six helps for fourteen underkeepers, and there were two deerkeepers and a boy to help them, as well as a groom, 'all under the demon Dadley'. Together they reared some 20,000 pheasants each season.

'Nobody liked Dadley: he got through sixty underkeepers and helps in just ten years – they just couldn't stick it. Yet he came highly recommended from the famous Hall Barn shoot in Buckinghamshire, which had the record for the number of pheasants shot in a day.' Of course, both Edward VII and George V often went shooting at Lord Burnham's Hall Barn and must have been impressed by Dadley's performance there.

'But the birds were always very poor at Windsor. The Prince of Wales – later Edward VIII – said that shooting there was "like knocking off chickens" and wanted no part of it.'

In July and August, when the young birds were put to wood, Charlie had to take his turn at nightwatching, one night in three. 'The first time, I went to relieve the underkeeper between Sandpit Gate and Ascot racecourse for a 10pm to 6am stint. After that I went straight home and said to the underkeeper with whom I lodged, next door to the headkeeper, "I'll have a nice cup of tea and go straight to bed now". But he said "Oh no you don't – you still have to do your normal work". So I carried on and did two days and a night with no bed. I can tell you I was mighty tired and nearly fell asleep over my spade when I tackled a bit of digging. But we did get an extra half-crown a night for watching.

'Talking about money, there was just one occasion when Dadley showed a spark of humanity. After I'd been at Windsor a while I was summoned to the office to get my travelling expenses from Six Mile Bottom to Windsor. I had come via Liverpool Street and Paddington and along the way had to pay five shillings for a taxi. Well, Major Taylor, the clerk, said "You should have gone on the Underground for tuppence." But blow me if Dadley didn't stick up for me. He was furious and banged his bowler hat down on the table, saying to Major Taylor: "Would you go on the Underground with a great tin trunk like his, and all the other gear, and not really knowing where you were going?" At that the Major gave me the full 15s to cover the whole journey without further question.

'At Windsor there wasn't really any way we could slip out the gate past Dadley, but one of my mates said it was safe to get out and in when the pips went on the radio as then we knew he was busy listening to the news. He never missed it. But we had to be ever so careful as Dadley was really crafty. He would gallop off on his grey horse at six in the morning to see two or three keepers and sometimes turn back within half an hour to surprise them, to see if they were smoking or sitting in the cab.

'One of the jobs Dadley's groom and me had to do was harrow down the very high bracken with the horses to make a clearing where the coops would go. Doing this we used to catch loads of rabbits, hitting them on the head with sticks as they all concentrated in the last little bit of cover. We were supposed to sell them to the butcher and give the proceeds to the estate, but we soon learned that the milkman wanted them for sixpence each.

'Another example of Dadley's vicious streak was when I had a whitlow and had to go on my bike to visit the Doctor at Winkfield, who put my arm in a sling and told me I was very run down – I'd lost a stone in three months. But when I went back that swine Dadley snatched the sling off and told me I was skiving.

'Another time he told me to milk a cow till it was really dry and then take it on a lead to Bracknell Market – seven miles away! So off I went through the forest, and before long the wretched thing had thrown me over a few times. But enough was enough. I managed to get the beast over and then it behaved itself.

'Anyway, I got there in the end, and for all my trouble Dadley had given me just one shilling – exactly the right amount to buy a pint of beer for myself and one for Ward the groom who was sent to pick me up in a pony and cart.

'Perhaps the last straw came when I was counting the game into the larder. One day I made it 1,104 and Dadley said "You are wrong – it's one less than 1,100". When I protested he said: "What do you know – you're just a boy", and I had to do it all over again. It was still exactly 1,104, but do you know, he never apologised.

'So I gave a month's notice and Dadley said I could change my mind at any time. But he did also say that he would try to get me another job, so off we went to Crufts again. As a result I ended up going to Frensham Park in Surrey, to work as beatkeeper for Richard Combe of the brewers Watney, Combe and Reed. He was really tickled by my name being Charlie South as he already had a second gardener called Charlie North and a farm labourer called Charlie West. Now, he said, he would look for a Charlie East "to get the full set".

'This was a much better job altogether. I had thirty-eight bob a week to start and this soon rose to £2, plus a suit of clothes a year and wonderful lodgings – within a few months I'd put that stone back on again. It was a far cry from Windsor, where I had only bread and marge and beetroot for supper, and where the only time we had meat was when a deer was run over once or twice a year.'

At Frensham the three keepers reared only 800 pheasants each year and some three or four hundred were shot over about three days. 'But there was plenty of duck shooting on Frensham Little Pond. However, one day when we were out in a boat Mr Combe nearly shot me in the head: it frightened him so much he declared "No more" and we all went home.

'There was also the traditional Boxing Day coot shoot on Frensham Big Pond. Anyone could go, even working men, as long as they paid the five shillings each. We shot scores and scores between us. The coots were very numerous at all seasons and during an open winter the water was sometimes fairly black with them.

'The Guns, a score or more, would assemble at the pond hotel and about half would go in boats in line to drive the pond while the rest were posted ashore. The total bag was usually about 150 plus a few duck. The "fixture" was discontinued after December 1931.'

Charlie thoroughly enjoyed his two and a half years at Frensham, but it came to an end when his father died – when he went home for the funeral he was offered his father's job at Six Mile Bottom. Thus, at the age of twenty-one, Charlie returned to take over the Weston Colville beat, 'thick woods and heavy land, not a good part of the estate'. The heavy land was a great disadvantage as wild partridges were then the main interest and they always thrive best on light, well-drained soil.

Charlie's first main task was tackling the considerable vermin problem and he caught twenty foxes in the first year. He followed a tip from an old Hampshire keeper and 'put out a bed of six gins with a stinkin' ol' cat in the middle of 'em'.

Partridge nests had to be checked religiously, of course, and in this a headkeeper would usually check up on his underkeepers – so would an interested employer. Remarkably, Charlie still has two of his maps from the 1930s, each recording details such as the number of eggs laid in each nest, number hatched etc. Proudly he recalls the day when his headkeeper and employer, Capt. Cunningham-Reid, came round in the Rolls Royce to check on his records. 'Right', said the Captain, 'according to this map there should be a nest under that telegraph pole.' And there was. He then proceeded to check just three more nests, and without further ado departed, satisfied that all was in order. The beat was obviously in the hands of a competent man.

Poaching was not a great problem in this very rural area until just after the war when food was rationed and, as Charlie said, 'everyone was really hungry'. The proliferation of cars aggravated the situation, but the keepers took the registration numbers and passed them on to the police to secure many convictions. Charlie used to carry a knuckleduster in his pocket, though he never actually used it. When he was given it by another, older keeper it still had two spikes on it, but Charlie decided to file these off in case he got into trouble with the law.

Charlie's reputation grew steadily and in 1950 he was made headkeeper on the retirement of Coot, then in charge of nine men. In those days Six Mile Bottom was a private shoot and there was a constant stream of guests for Charlie to look after.

I asked Charlie which of the many guest Guns had been his favourites. Quick as a flash and with a knowing grin, he replied: 'The ones who gave me the most money.'

Among the most famous visitors was prolific novelist Barbara Cartland, who often came to watch her two sons (McCorquodales) shoot. 'She spent most of her time feeding Lord Louis (Mountbatten) chocolates', said Charlie's wife, Dorcas. 'She was a great talker and very familiar with all the guests.'

Like other headkeepers, Charlie also accompanied his boss to many other shoots, to act as loader. 'The best I ever went to was Helmsley in Yorkshire, with Mr Noel, the Captain's son and present owner. Noel had thirty-inch guns and full-load cartridges as well as all the gear you could want, yet still found shooting difficult there. They didn't kill one in seven between them. The birds were so high you could hear the pellets rattling their wings as they flew on unscathed. And one of the other guests – Sir Kenneth Keith, a really good Shot – said "I'm giving up, I can't hit anything". The Helmsley shoot was then run by Prince Radziwill and Lord Ashburton, and didn't they spend some money on it and their guests!

'One of my most memorable shooting days was when I had the pleasure to load for Edward Douglas-Home, brother of the famous playwright, William. To my great surprise, he shot a hundred cock pheasants and never missed one: that was some shooting, I can tell you.'

Charlie continued to live at Six Mile Bottom after his retirement in 1974, and died there in October 1993.

Almost a Fixture

———— ooooo ————

The only trouble with spending all or most of your working life on one estate is that you tend to get handed down with the fixtures and fittings and no one generation of owners or sportsmen can truly appreciate your total commitment. And never has this been more true than in the case of Allan Cameron, whose service on the Burnside estate, near Forfar, spanned seventy years, from the age of fourteen to eighty-four. No few words of thanks from any individual could ever do justice to this extraordinary devotion to duty, but at least now it is properly recognised for posterity within these pages.

When Allan was born, at Motherwell, Lanarkshire, on 15 February 1908, his father was not a gamekeeper, but he could hardly have come from a more distinguished keeping family. His great-grandfather, grandfather and two uncles had all, in turn, been headkeeper for the Duke of Argyll.

'I was the eldest of five children and father was one of ten. There was very little work in the area, so he had to content himself with driving a horse-drawn cart selling lemonade around Motherwell, where he met mother. But he was always on the lookout for a keeper's job. Eventually his persistence paid off. When I was three he became single-handed gamekeeper for the Barrs, brewers at Harburn, near West Calder, Midlothian.'

While still at school, Allan started to help father on the grouse moor, but did not get any pocket money. The only time he received any reward was when he went beating, for which he received half-a-crown, and a cold pie and lime juice for lunch.

The other beaters were generally the four shepherds employed by the Barrs. 'But when needed, father had to help them too, with the shearing. It was big blackface sheep country.'

During World War I Allan's father was away in the Royal Garrison Artillery. 'From 1916 to 1919 mother took us away from the very lonely house we had at Harburn to stay with grandmother at Motherwell. Times were very hard then and I used to queue for hours at the shops for a quarter pound of margarine, sometimes only to find that it was all gone when it was my turn.'

In 1919 Allan's father returned to his job at Harburn and the family rejoined him there. 'From then on he 'ad to spend six months of the year helpin' the shepherds and he didn't like it.

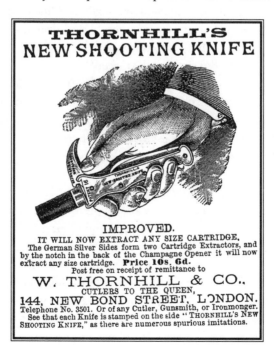

Our lighting was paraffin lamps and our heating was mainly peat cut from the moor. Father's wages was only a guinea a week.'

In those days there was a lot more game at Harburn. For example, Allan recalls seeing a flock of over 150 black grouse there. 'They're canny birds and always used to fly back over the beaters, so father would give 'em a shot or two to help send them over the Guns.

'I helped with the heather burning too, and I remember some of the fires gettin' well away, but not with father – he was pretty careful. It was the shepherds who let 'em go. Once one set a whole hill on fire and he was away to his bed. I always remember that, because next mornin' the chauffeur was out gatherin' the abandoned curlews' and other eggs for the big house. Officially, burnin' was allowed up to 20 April then.

'One of my jobs was to feed the dogs – mostly on porridge, none of these fancy biscuits. There was a great big potful boiled up outside. This kept 'em goin' for two days. We also gave them rabbits and cracklin' – a big block of dried beef you hacked pieces off.'

But despite his early experience, Allan did not go straight into keepering when he left school at the age of fourteen. For a few months he worked for Edinburgh Corporation, who had market gardens at West Calder. There he earned 7/6d a day, 'pulling berries – mostly gooseberries, blackcurrants and redcurrants, and later on all sorts of vegetables.

'Then father got a job as keeper/overseer for Widow Robertson at Burnside, just outside Forfar. At the same time I was taken on as keeper's assistant, in November 1922. I was to remain there for the rest of my working life, single-handed after father died. I'd just as soon 'ave been a gardener but, although there were four on the estate, there were no vacancies at the time. They had six greenhouses and grew everythin' from peaches to melons, but now it's all rack and ruin.

'Everybody helped one another in those days. For example, when the big garden was dug we all 'ad to come in and help for the day – even the chauffeur. And when the hedges were cut we all joined in. That took seven of us two and a half days using ordinary hand shears. Our field hedges and fences always had a yard of cover either side for the game. There was an agreement with the farmers for this. Now the scientists call this conservation headlands and are trying to get everyone on it, but it's nothing new, only forgotten.'

As Allan's father had wide-ranging responsibilities at Burnside he was paid a good wage – £3 a week. 'He also had a free house, light, milk and five loads of coal a year. And these were wagon-loads too – sometimes 30cwt or more – drawn by horse from Forfar station. Sometimes the estate bought a whole lot from the mine because the other houses had some too. As part of their agreement, the farmers had to do three days a year free carting for the estate.

'At first I was paid £1 a week and my work was all on rabbits. The hill was nearly bare as the road with 'em. Twice a week the chauffeur took the snared rabbits to Stewart's fish shop in Forfar. But in the hot weather, when they wouldn't keep, I had to cycle down with them over my handlebars every night when I came in from work. All the heads were tied together so that they didn't do into the spokes of the front wheel, but I still wasted a few bikes with rabbits. I ruined a Rudge in eighteen months. I used to 'ave so many on it I could hardly pedal – even with my legs wide apart.

'I also used to go out with father to get game for a hamper, which was regularly sent to the family in Edinburgh, or to their London home. A typical lot would include two pair rabbits, two brace pheasants, a woodcock or two, and always several wild duck, as well as occasional grouse.'

ooooo

After the Camerons had been at Burnside for three years, the estate was bought by the Maitland family. 'Mr Ramsay Maitland came from the Woodbank Estate, Loch Lomond. He was a nice gentleman who got his Sir when his brother died.

'That first year he came – 1925 – there was a good stock of game, but we shot so many we had to start rearing in 1926. We always had two-day shoots, starting 8/9 November. The first day would be on the hill, but there were only a few grouse. It was mostly pheasants and quite a few woodcock – we 'ad nineteen twice.

'Like everybody else at the time, we mixed the chick food. For the first ten days we chopped the usual hardboiled eggs – but only the yolks, though I'm not sure why. There was also Gilbertson and Page's fine biscuit meal and a special drying-off meal. Later on we used chopped rabbit meat and rolled it in your hands with the dryin' meal as the birds didn't like anythin' wet. But it was mainly for the separation really. The young pheasant was wrapped up in cotton wool in those days.

'The birds liked perch too. We chopped the fish up just the same after they was boiled, boned and gutted, but you had to pull the spines off. As the birds got bigger they could take great chunks of fish. We had loads from the lake, so it was free food.

'When the birds went to wood they had mostly wheat and kibbled maize. It was very hard work taking the birds out. With a rope round the neck, two of us would carry two coops, each with a hen and sixteen to eighteen chicks in it. A whole day of that back and forth was enough for anyone. We were out at first light and only stopped when we tripped over in the dark.'

In many ways the birds fared better than the keepers and beaters. 'But they did kill a blackfaced sheep for us at each shoot. We had shepherd's pie one day and mutton stew the next.' Meanwhile, the Guns lunched well at the big house.

Before World War II, 'poachers used to come out on the train from Dundee for the rabbits, but that line's away now. There's not been that many poachers from Forfar and we've generally known who they are. We used to watch quite a bit at night when the moon was up, but I'd not hide if a vehicle came along; I'd still parade along the road to give 'em some idea that there was someone about. The main thing was listening and using your eyes.

'Sir Ramsay (Colonel) Maitland was a right military man and when the war started got us all to join the Local Defence Volunteers. At first all we had was shotguns and his big rifle he used to shoot elephants and tigers with in India. Our observation post was on a hillock lookin' down on Lunan Bay, between Montrose and Arbroath, where they thought any invaders would come in. When it was clear you could see the sea glitterin' in the moonlight.

'We used to just turn out when the siren went. Up here we used to 'ave a road block – just barrels filled with stones: it would hardly stop a bullock let alone a tank. But eventually we got organised a bit and had .303 Ross rifles, not that they were very good.

'One day there were three of us on duty and the siren went. It was a bit misty but you could hear the bombers comin' and I was goin' to have a shot with the elephant rifle as one plane was that low. When the engine noise dropped you could hear the wind whistlin' through his struts. But the mist was just too thick and try as I might I could na see him, and he went on to drop two bombs. It was very disappointing. I tell you that dumdum bullet would certainly have made a hole in him. Old Sir Ramsay took that rifle out stalking and once shot a roe deer. It made a hole so big my father gutted the deer through it!'

At the end of 1940 Allan was posted to Normanby Hall, in

Lincolnshire, and stayed in that county on Bofors guns up to 1945. 'We were mostly round Scunthorpe defending the steel-works.

'The only narrow escape I had was when a plane dropped this Molotov cocktail stuff all about us. If it had been the normal high explosive I wouldn't be here now telling you this. But we did manage to shoot a Heinkel bomber – it came down two miles away. The people there were so delighted they brought us out all kinds of cakes. You'd 'ave thought we'd save the lives of everyone in Scunthorpe.'

It was during the war, in 1944, that Allan married Georgina, 'an undercook in the big house at Burnside. There always used to be two Christmas parties for the estate workers then. One was for married women and their families and the other one for married men and single staff. Everyone got a present and there was a good turkey meal.'

Shooting continued at Burnside during the war, though on a much-reduced scale, 'because there was only father and the chauffeur left to look after things. When the Poles were in Forfar they planted a wood for us, which became known as Polish Wood. Father always used to say that the best tip he had was one shilling from a Polish officer.

'They was mostly all good Shots in the old days. Lord Southesk and Lord Dalhousie were the best I can recall. And when I was beating at Drumailbo I always remember the pile of dead par-tridges laying around Prince Philip. But that was one of the great partridge shoots in Angus and they did rear quite a few.'

When it came to pests few men were more experienced than Allan. 'In the old days the biggest vermin was the small grass weasel, so before we set the coops out we liked the rearing field grazed as short as possible. But by the time we'd finished the grass was way up. Although you couldn't see it, you always knew it was a weasel because you'd see a pheasant jumping up trying to fly. All you could do was wait for a squeak when it got a bird and then blast at the final flutter and hope that the intruder was killed. Even the young weasels could catch the young gamebirds.

'Sparrowhawks were easier to get as they'd nearly always come back to the same coop as long as there were birds there. All you had to do was wait in hiding and shoot them. We used to go round their nests in the woods too. Father used pole traps when they were legal but I never did.

'The kestrel was the worst to get as he'd come in and hover anywhere in the field, so it was hard to ambush. Tawny owls sometimes took the head off a young bird and then we'd trap them in a gin.'

Allan has never had any trouble with mink, 'but I did suffer through a brood of wild ferrets, at Burnside just when duck shooting had been put back to 1 September. The release pen was by the big house and one day I found dead pheasants all round by the wire. I ran back to the lodge for my gun and waited for ages, but saw nothing. So I lifted out all the dead birds except five, which I set by Fenn traps just outside the pen because I thought it was stoats.

'In the evening, after a day's shoot, I went back and there in the traps were a bitch ferret and two young dog ferrets. I kept the traps set and ended up with ten young ferrets as well as the old bitch. I never did see the old dog ferret there. But about two months later, a good bit away, one of my snared rabbits was broken open, so I set a trap there and caught him, too.

'Now there's hardly any predator control for miles around because all the old estates have been broken up and most of the full-time keepers are gone. This is partly why all the capers [capercaillies] are gone. The worst thing now is so many foxes getting the eggs and young on the ground. There are a lot more badgers to take them too.

'We always used to get capers round here, but once we shot eight hens in a day and that was the ruination of it. It was the first year a syndicate took the shooting and they were only allowed one bird each, but one greedy Gun shot four! He said he couldn't resist them. But when they stopped shooting them altogether you could walk right up to them in the trees, so that didn't help. They became so tame they were vulnerable to poachers and predators.'

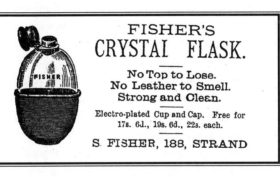

Despite so many years' experience, Allan admits that you never stop learning. Even in his last rearing season he was puzzled by predation. 'It was summer 1991 and I had 200 five-week-old poults. On the second morning seventeen were lyin' dead with a bite on top of the head. I thought it was a weasel or rat, so I went home and got a tin of Cymag and gassed all the rabbit holes round about.

'But the next morning there was another ten lyin' dead. So I told the boss I'd put the rest in the pen by the big house. The first night I waited right through till I could na see and the only thing I saw was a hedgehog. But he didn't go in the pop-holes so I let him be.

'Two days later some more birds were killed in the same way, so I stayed to watch all day. Just as it was getting dark a hedgehog appeared and went in the pop-hole, so I shot him. I watched a bit more, then went home.

'Next morning there was nothing, so I thought that was the end of it. But two days later there were more birds dead and I shot another hedgehog. That really was the finish of it.

'A lot of people just won't believe that hedgehogs behave in this way, but I've had them attacking fowls before. They went for their rear ends in the coops, where the hens couldn't defend themselves. Afterwards you always had to kill the birds as they were torn and bleeding. The hedgehogs were also very bad with eggs.'

That Allan was able to continue keepering so actively into his 85th year (he stopped altogether on 23 May 1992) was certainly exceptional. Officially he retired at sixty-five and from then on was supposed to be part-time, 'but it continued more or less the same as there was no one else to do it'. Indeed, his loyalty was remarkable given his disability.

Allan first broke his leg at the age of twenty when he rode over some potholes and came off his Coventry Eagle Flying 350 motorcycle. 'There were no steering dampers to save you then when you got a wobble.' Unfortunately for him, neither did they have X-rays in those days so Forfar Infirmary simply, 'propped me up in sandbags for seven or eight weeks and hoped for the best. But it was never set right and two years later I broke it again while walking a turnip field for partridges.' And not surprisingly, when he broke it a third time, in a rabbit hole after World War II, the leg became steadily worse. Now it is very debilitating, with the main bone pressing sideways and down over the ankle.

Despite the weakness, Allan remained 'motorbike daft. I finished up with a 500 Norton just after the war. Then I bought a little car – a Ford 8.'

Allan's wife died in 1990 and now he lives with one of his three children, having decided to vacate the keeper's house at Burnside. From the window of aptly named 'Burnside View', on the outskirts of Forfar, he can see the hills over which he walked so many times, and reflect on the contrasting ways of generations. Apart from the Robertsons, he has served three generations of Maitland, and there is no doubting that he liked the old, more gentlemanly and far less commercialised days best. Although there is now no keeper in the family, Allan's only son having taken a different path, there is no doubting that the name of Cameron will echo about the hills of Angus for many years to come.

KING OF THE GAMEKEEPERS

---- ∞∞∞ ----

I n his position as headkeeper for the late Earl Mountbatten at Broadlands, Harry Grass acquired a reputation as one of the greatest gamekeepers this century, and the popular press christened him 'King of the Gamekeepers'. This was indeed a great tribute to a man whose family has been the most famous in the entire history of gamekeeping. At their peak, there were 103 members of the Grass family working as keepers across the land at one time.

Harry's grandfather, father and all five uncles were game-keepers. His father and Uncle Harry were keepers on the Earl of Durham's Lambton Castle Estate, where Harry was born, at Houghton Gate, on 4 December 1908. He started work there as kennel boy at the age of fourteen, and under headkeeper Skelton his main job was to feed and exercise the fifty to sixty labradors, spaniels and flatcoats. But before that, while still at school, he used to sit in the woods with a .410, keeping watch over his father's pheasants.

One day his father said to him: 'Look here, if you're going to be a keeper always remember one thing – what you are looking after belongs to someone else.' Today, Harry says 'Too many people help themselves. In my time, if the boss said to me "Have a pheasant" I said thank you very much, but that was that.'

Harry's starting wage was 14s a week and after the first year he was given the keeper's uniform of a frocktail coat, breeches, boxcloth leggings and a trilby, though some keepers wore bowlers then.

At first, Harry was assigned as helper to beatkeeper Jim Hawkins, whose word was law. 'And in those days you only spoke to his lordship if you were spoken to first.'

As one of a team of twelve keepers, Harry stayed at Lambton for about a year and a half. Then one day his mother received word that Mr H. Wigmore of The Hermitage, Chester-le-Street was willing to take him on as underkeeper. So away he went, into lodgings with the head groom, to gain valuable experience.

The Hermitage had a good mixed pheasant and partridge shoot, but more unusual was its 1,400-acre (566ha) rookery, shot once a year over about a fortnight. This provided excellent sport, much of it with shotguns as well as rifles, and Harry remembers how one evening they shot over a hundred rooks on the wing!

Then Harry returned to Lambton for four years as second keeper on the Penshaw beat, until one day headkeeper Thomas Scott said to him: 'If you want to learn your job properly then you should go down to East Anglia.' Harry agreed and Scott eventually found him a position as one of seven beatkeepers

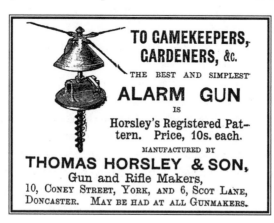

with Lord Henniker, at Thornham Hall, Thornham Magna, near Eye, Suffolk. 'Henniker was known as "the little old man", but he was a good Shot and a well-known field trial judge. I really enjoyed my four years with him, and during that time I met and married Stella Mayes of Thornham Magna.

'At Henniker's each man was responsible for 100–150 coops. I had to walk a mile to the rearing field and be there by 6am. We had to mix all the pheasant food four times a day – at 7am, 11am, 3pm and 7pm, from when the birds were day-olds till they went to wood at six weeks. We had to stop on the rearing field till the birds were shut up and we were lucky if we were home by 10pm. You can imagine how tired we were as we trudged back home in the dark, with the owls hooting all about and every shadow regarded with suspicion.

'We also had to feed the hens and move the coops onto fresh ground every day. And each keeper had to run 50–60 traps.'

Harry remembers his time at Thornham with great affection. 'I knew it was a caring place from the day I arrived, when the headkeeper met me at the railway station with his pony and cart. As we drove the five miles to his house, travelling down narrow country roads, I saw thatched cottages with pink and cream-washed walls and I got the feeling that I had moved back in time by something like fifty years for I had not seen anything quite like it before.

'Over the next few days I met the rest of the keepers and, although we had dialect difficulties, and did so for quite some time, we all spoke "keepers' language". But I was in a completely different world: this was true country, untouched by anything modern – craftsmen carried out their duties using methods which had long vanished in the part of the North I had known. I saw men making large farm wagons and tumbrils, and farm methods and cropping were not the same. There were no heavy

Shire horses and no hills, only flat ground. Even the weather was different, and, unless my memory is at fault, all the summers seemed to be warm and dry.

'The estate was in effect a country factory and everyone in the locality was employed by it, men of all professions, including foresters, sawyers, carpenters, painters and farmworkers. They even made their own bricks and field drains in moulds. The estate was self-supporting in every way and was owned and governed by a true country gentleman.

'Shooting took pride of place on the estate and dominated four days every other week. And during the Christmas period, when the boys were home from school, every day saw small parties enjoying the sport. Beaters were drawn from other departments on the estate so it really was a "family" outing.

'In those days the shooting men gave the keepers a party in one of the "locals" – there were two on the estate and it was held at each alternately. Those who had assisted the keepers – loaders, village policemen, head carpenter and so on – were also invited, and it was a time for everyone to let their hair down.

'Another party was held for the entire staff in the large, rambling servants' hall at the mansion, where all the married staff went for tea and all the single staff went for the evening's entertainment – a mixture of dancing and singing helped along with fairly liberal mugfuls of what was known locally as "owld beer", which either made you a little worse for wear or sobered you up, depending on what state you were in to begin with.

'Around midnight the family would come in and wish us all the compliments of the season. We would then all join hands to sing "Auld Lang Syne", and we meant every word of it.'

Harry turned his beat into the best on the estate and when John Palmer retired Harry took over as a second keeper. Lord Henniker also said that when headkeeper John Chandler retired, Harry would take his place – but eleven years was too long for the ambitious Mr Grass to wait.

'One day a gentleman farmer came to see me and asked me to head a small two-keeper shoot between Bury St Edmunds and Newmarket. So off I went and made it the best shoot of its size in Suffolk, if not in England. And when the day came for me to resign, the owner, Mr Gittus, actually cried.

'The agent of Lord Milford of Dalham Hall, near Market, came to see me and invited me to go there as headkeeper. And I am pleased to say that I made it the finest pheasant shoot in all

England. One day 1,200 pheasants came out from one drive – the North Field Belt – and the seven Guns killed only sixty-eight birds, such was their quality.'

Harry regarded Lord Milford as 'a great man', but 'he was so different from his son, Major Philipps. Matters came to a head one day when the Major was rude to my wife; I threatened to smack him in the mouth and decided to leave.'

Another job came along quickly, taking Harry to be the head of two keepers working for Lady Janet Bailey of Lake in Wiltshire. There his reputation continued to grow and after only one year Lord Mountbatten's agent came to see him and asked him to go to Broadlands in Hampshire as headkeeper.

Harry was 'signed on' by Lady Mountbatten, who at first declared that he could not spend much money as the shoot was at rock bottom. Not surprisingly, Harry, in his typically direct way, said 'I must have sufficient funds, but most of all I want my own way of doing things'. Fortunately, Lady Mountbatten agreed and said that Harry would be answerable to no one except her, not even the agent.

As a result, on their first day, less than a year later, they killed more pheasants than in the whole of the previous season. Lady Mountbatten joined the party on the last drive before lunch and said to her husband: 'How are you getting on, dear?' He replied: 'We've already discovered one thing – Grass is not going to stand any nonsense.'

Thus the shoot's big build-up began, and it wasn't long before royal guests came from all over Europe to enjoy Broadlands' much talked about sport, at a time when big bags were still very much in vogue.

On Harry's best day ever, in 1968, they killed 2,139 pheasants on just four drives, and Prince Charles bagged 500! As usual, Harry blew his whistle to signal no more shooting after each drive, but after the last a single shot rang out. Harry told me 'I was so shocked, as my word was law and everyone knew it. So I marched over to the Guns to find out who the guilty party was. To my great surprise it was Prince Charles, and before I could say anything he said : "I'm sorry, but I'd killed 499 when the whistle went and I don't suppose I'll ever do that again." Still rather cross, I said to the prince: "Don't do it again, sir." "What?", he asked, "firing after the whistle?" "No, shoot 500 pheasants", I quipped, allowing a slight smile to creep across my face.'

According to Harry, Prince Charles was then a much better Shot than the more experienced Prince Philip. When Prince Philip first went to Broadlands they shot 1,417 and he said to Harry: 'I bet you'll never do that again.' But Harry proudly recalls: 'The very next time he came we killed 1,600. There was no way I would allow standards to slip.'

Another famous guest was motoring mogul Henry Ford. One day he shot dangerously, at a partridge into the faces of the approaching beaters. Harry spun round to Lord Mountbatten and said 'Shall I go and warn him, sir?' The Earl replied: 'No, I'll get Lord Brabourne [Lord Mountbatten's son-in-law] to do it; he's a bit more diplomatic than you.'

Lord Mountbatten was 'a fair Shot', but to Harry he was 'a good employer, a good master and a real friend'. They travelled extensively together, Harry driving his master many hundreds of miles to other shoots. 'We often stopped off at his London house on the way, and we always had the same lunch – no discrimination.'

One famous shoot which they visited frequently was Sandringham, and it was on the royal estate that Harry mentioned to Lord Mountbatten that he had his retirement papers through. The Earl looked horrified and said to Harry: 'You're not going to retire: not only are you my keeper, but you are also my friend.' So Harry stayed on.

Lord Mountbatten's death at the hands of the IRA was a bitter blow to Harry, and with his friend and employer's passing the old keeper really lost his enthusiasm for almost everything. His sadness was as deep as his roots in keepering and he still remembered vividly how he joined the estate's other three heads of department in standing guard over Lord Mountbatten's coffin at the mansion. 'When you walked in you could have heard a pin drop, and when I looked up there were ladies with tears in their eyes.'

The estate passed to Lord Romsey, the Earl's grandson, who wanted to get rid of Broadlands' reputation as a 'blunderbuss' shoot, and instead concentrate on quality birds in smaller numbers. Of course, the young lord found it extremely difficult to follow in the footsteps of such a popular and loved employer. Harry found him 'altogether a different kettle of fish, and when, after a year or so, he suggested that I might retire, I did not find the decision difficult'.

Harry was given a small cottage at Broadlands for the rest of his life, along with a small pension. He started to grow a few tomatoes and cucumbers and sometimes went to watch on shooting days, occasionally 'waving a white flag to get the birds up a bit'. And each Thursday he still drove his old Ford the seven miles to Romsey to help out in the gunshop there.

Much of Harry's sound advice was once regularly recorded in the pages of *Shooting Times*, the editor having asked him to contribute a monthly page in the late seventies and early eighties. He always wrote in longhand and persuaded one of the ladies in the Broadlands estate office to type each piece, but his style was excellent and needed very little editing.

Harry's subject matter ranged far and wide, from rearing to roosting, from predation to tipping. The biggest tip he ever received was '£40 from a foreigner, but the average in my last few years at Broadlands was £10. And royals always tipped much in line with the other guests. As is customary, I shared the tips out with the other keepers at the end of the season, unless there was a particularly good day, when it was done immediately. In the old days at Lambton we always thought that the headkeeper kept more than his fair share when it came to pay-out time. I suppose all keepers suspect their bosses.'

Harry was particularly renowned for his success in dealing with poachers. And he had to be specially vigilant at Broadlands, which is so easily accessible by a number of major roads and only a few miles from Southampton and other towns.

While working for Sir Arthur Wood at The Hermitage a poacher stabbed him in the thigh and lower leg and he needed ten stitches. A friend advised him to learn how to wrestle and box, and this he did with a vengeance, eventually becoming one of the most feared keepers of his generation. He took lessons once or twice a week from the amateur champion of Cumberland and Westmorland style wrestling. When he could pin down and throw his tutor he went to another amateur champion to learn how to box, becoming proficient at that, too. He was a match for anyone.

Harry was only eleven when he gave evidence against a poacher for the first time. He was on his way home from school when he saw one of the Lambton keepers chasing a man with a .410. Later the headkeeper was consulted and it was decided that, despite his tender years, Harry was sufficiently mature to identify the poacher in court. And afterwards, the magistrate congratulated him on the clear way he gave evidence.

As the years went by Harry became increasingly tough with the many poachers he apprehended and had no hesitation in 'giving them a good hiding'. Once a gypsy threatened Harry with a knife, but the fearless keeper had no trouble in seizing the weapon. 'I cut off the tip of his nose with it and said "There, every time you look in the mirror you'll remember me and think twice about coming here again!"'

At Henniker's the keepers went nightwatching in groups of three, their shifts being from dusk till 1am, and 1am till dawn. Anyone caught was taken to the local police station. Harry and his colleagues never called in the police to help apprehend poachers, as is the modern, more cautious, practice.

At Henry Bell's, Harry once found a revolver left behind by a poacher, whom he recognised as the local Italian ice-cream seller. 'When I went in and slapped the gun down on his counter you should have seen the look on his face.' Harry himself never carried a revolver, but he always has a home-made truncheon.

Despite all his fighting expertise, Harry did not go to the front in the last war. Instead, he was a sergeant in the Home Guard at Bury St Edmunds. The closest he ever came to hostilities was when two planes crashed on his shoot, 'one of ours and one of theirs, and both pilots were killed'.

However, he saw death twice in the shooting field. One accident took place at Lord Iveagh's famous Elveden shoot near Thetford, when Harry was loading for Major Philipps. The loader for a neighbouring Gun accidentally shot the second keeper in the stomach and he was dead before they reached him. Later they learned that this was the first time the careless man had acted as a loader.

While such horrific incidents persuaded lesser men to take up safer, Harry never wavered in his love of the keepering life. Not only was he the friend and confidant of kings and commoners, he was himself a king, the absolute ruler of fine sporting estates and the terror of those who would steal his game.

He died in May 1990.

BRIDESHEAD REVISITED

⌐ ∞∞∞ ¬

I n the 1980s, independent television made its blockbusting series 'Brideshead Revisited' at Castle Howard, and the headkeeper then had to help keep adoring spectators off estate roads so that filming could continue. But at least the commotion did not appear to affect the pheasants, so Lord Howard, ironically Chairman of the BBC, could continue with his celebrated sport.

Castle Howard's rise to shooting prominence was largely due to the loyalty and skill of this one man: headkeeper Stanley Ware, who spent most of his working life nurturing the game-birds of Yorkshire.

Stanley was born on 5 May 1918 in the tiny village of Gillamoor near Kirbymoorside, Yorkshire. His father was a rabbit catcher for much of the year, mostly September to April; otherwise he would break up stones in the quarries and dig trenches for water pipes at 3d a yard.

Most of the rabbits were ferreted or caught in gin traps and snares; only a few were shot because a couple of good, 'clean' rabbits would fetch 1/6d whereas a couple of shot ones made only between 8d and 10d. 'But father didn't get all that', said Stanley. 'He was employed by Colonel Holt and his estate paid him 3d for each rabbit caught. Most rabbits were crated and put on the train for London markets. But there were a lot of rabbits then and a lot of people were worse off than us. And in the Great War, when father was rejected by the Army on account of his feet, the Government sent him all over the place to keep the rabbits down on many estates.'

When he was still at school at Gillamoor, Stanley started to become interested in keepering through his grandfather, who was a beatkeeper for Lord Feversham at Nawton Towers. But Stanley had to walk the eight miles to visit him.

At the age of twelve, Stanley had his first experience as a beater, for Colonel Holt on the Ravenswick estate, near Kirbymoorside. The pay was 2s a day, but beaters had to take their own lunch and cold tea in a bottle as there were no flasks in those days. Very often Stanley was given one of the easy jobs as a stop because he knew the ground well through going there with his father to catch rabbits.

Stanley was pleased to leave school at the age of fourteen, to get out into the fresh air and help his father with his work. He did not have to set the ginns because he was particularly good at snaring – 'The best place to snare was where the rabbits ran across a grass field to feed in a field of roots. It was quite easy to spot their runs in the long grass, especially after frost.' In return for this work, Stanley received free board and lodging with his parents, but no pay.

Four years later the headkeeper at Castle Howard asked Stanley's father, who caught rabbits there, if he knew of a lad who wanted to take up keepering. Not surprisingly, he suggested his own son, and thus in 1936 began an association which has lasted to this day.

His employer was the late Lord Grimthorpe, who then leased about half of the Castle Howard estate. Headkeeper was Joe Durno, 'a damn good man', and Stanley was paid about 10s a week, of which 5s went to his aunt for lodging with her at the appropriately named Gunthorpe village on Castle Howard estate.

He started at the end of February and one of his main tasks was killing vermin. The main method of catching crows was to place eggs on a tree stump to entice the birds down and lure them into a trap. 'But foxes were taboo. Being an MFH, Lord Grimthorpe would have sacked us if he had seen us shoot one. But if one became a real nuisance it had to be a three o'clock in the morning job!'

In the late thirties farming was more sympathetic towards game and wildlife. There were many more hedgerows and no spraying so the partridges could usually be left to fend for themselves. The keeper's main work was concerned with rearing large numbers of pheasants, and that really got underway in April when rabbit catching was finished with . 'At home we rarely ate rabbit and mother always had to disguise it in the cooking pot. But father always knew it was there. You can hardly blame him for turning his nose up at it, having had to gut them all day long.

'Our broody hens were bought from farms and local people – everybody kept a few hens – for 2s 6d each, and put into sitting boxes with six compartments. The hen's quota of eggs depended on her size and varied from eighteen to twenty.

'Every morning the hens were taken out of their boxes and tethered by one leg to a stick, and each hen had to be put back onto her own nest; after a few days they got used to this. When a hen was taken off the nest, the keeper had to put his hands under the bird and move her back slightly to lift her feet from the eggs so that she would not drag them forward and break them on the board. Then the hen was passed to another man, who put her on her tether.

'Before and during sitting the hens were dusted with louse powder to kill any fleas they might be carrying. Infested birds would shift about relentlessly on the eggs and break quite a few.

'During the first part of incubation the hens were allowed only a short time off the eggs, but as time went on they were allowed longer spells off duty. When they were finally put back on the eggs we went round with shovel and hose to clean up any mess they had made or food not eaten. And we always turned the drinking bowls upside down to keep vermin away.

'The siting of the sitting boxes was very important. Too much direct sun would make the hens shift about on the nest, and even sometimes rise from the eggs, which would then be chilled. They had to be placed a few inches above ground level in case of heavy rain, ideally on a ridge of sandy soil which was well drained. At the same time this made it a little bit easier for the keeper to remove the birds.

'This done, the nests were shaped with a rounded stone and lined with hay or dried grass into which hot eggs were placed. These were left with the hens for a couple of days to discover which were the best sitters. Some of the hens never took to the boxes after running around free on the farms. And we had to put a wire fence around the boxes to keep out dogs and foxes.

'While the hens were still sitting the rearing field had to be prepared, first by putting tunnel traps all around the hedgerows. Then we cut rides about a yard wide across the field to stand the coops in, twenty yards between the rows and twenty yards between each coop. All this covered several acres of land, which was rented from one of the tenant farmers.

'When the coops were first put out they were turned upside down and limewashed inside. Small runs were placed in front of the coops for the first few days. Then along came the rearing hut complete with pans, buckets and feeding bowls. And as soon as possible we had to find lots of dry wood to store under the hut in case of wet weather as all the food was boiled.

'By this time all the chicks were hatching out. When they had dried off under their broody they were taken to the rearing field in boxes, the hen in a sack. In each coop a hen had about eighteen chicks.

'Then we started boiling food. Eggs were cooked forty at a time and put through a fine sieve. Rice, kibbled maize, linseed and wheat were boiled too. This was all mixed up in the feeding bowl with scalded fine biscuit meal and finally dried off with barley meal and dusted with a tiny amount of Pheasant-tina spice to make the food taste better.

'After each feed the bowls were immediately put into boiling water as soft food soon went sour. The coops were moved onto fresh ground every day or two.

'Often the chicks became infested with gapes: these are little, pink worms which get into the windpipe and lungs, and if they are not treated up to half the birds could die. We would block up most of the air vents in the coop and use bellows to blow in some powder called Camlin, which the birds breathed in for a few minutes.

'At this time of year you were on the rearing field from six in the morning till the birds were shut up at night, and as the birds got older this became later: on very mild nights it could be eleven o'clock.

'With three keepers on this shoot, two were on the rearing field while the other went around the woods cutting rides with a scythe ready to receive the coops and in preparation for the birds' release.

'At four to five weeks old the birds were moved to cover. The night before they would be fastened in; we would place a sack under the coop and lift the thing bodily onto a cart, and as we had a horse to pull it we could reach wherever we wanted to go. The coops were placed out on the ride as on the rearing field, but the hens were facing in all directions so that they could give us warning when any vermin came in sight.

'The hens stayed in the wood for several weeks before being taken home. By this time they were in laying condition and sold

as laying hens for the same price as we gave for them.

'The keeper still had to boil the food and see the birds had plenty of water. His last job before going home for the night was to boil the food ready for the morning feed. At the same time he would see the birds had some grit, and light the hurricane lamps to keep the foxes away.

'From twelve weeks old the birds started to stray away from the coverts so then we used a dog to drive them back home.

'We had about four partridge days of 50–70 brace each and ten or so covert shoots with bags of 140–150 pheasants.

'Our beaters were paid 2s 6d a day and given a bottle of beer each. The lucky ones were given a cartridge bag to carry and for this they might get an extra half-crown each. One gentleman used to give a pound so everybody rushed for him.

'The poachers then were all local people as there was very little transport. But we had to be nightwatching from the start as they could still take a lot of birds. We used to take turns with neighbouring keepers to watch for these trouble-makers – one man in the Territorial Army used to knock off birds with his .303.

'When the shooting season was over we had hen pheasants to catch for the laying pens, about seven hens to each cock. This done, we started on the rabbit population as in those days there were so many of them. After some time at them with gins, snares, ferrets and guns, a lot of them would take to sitting out on top. These were dealt with by a few farm tenants and others who helped during the nesting season. The keeper drove the rabbits forward with dogs and hopefully they were shot by the people standard forward. But we still left snares and traps going until April.

'Then we started on carrion crows and magpies, which were sitting by this time. Tunnel traps were kept going for ground vermin.

'Early pheasants started to lay in April and English partridges early in May. We found as many of these as possible so we could put Renardine around the nests in cartridge cases to take away the scent of the birds, which otherwise might attract predators. On wet days we went to the shed to creosote the coops and sitting boxes.

'By the middle of May it was time to start all over again with the broody hens.'

This regime continued until January 1940, when Stanley was called up to join the Royal Artillery.

After the war Lord Grimthorpe lost his lease at Castle Howard. Stanley worked single-handed for three doctors on another part of the estate.

Boxing Day was 'the big one', when wives and families always turned out to beat 'and I had a job to keep 'em all in line. And it was a good job I had a few Christmas boxes, as tips were few then. The most you would ever receive was £1 but I would say I never really had a good tip in my life. They didn't realise what a keeper had to do to put a few shots over them.'

During his eighteen years with the doctors, Stanley lived in a rented house at nearby Welburn, having married during the war.

Then came a telephone call from Mr (later Lord) George Howard of Castle Howard, asking him to go for interview with a view to replacing the headkeeper Joe Durno, who had unexpectedly taken a job as a milkman. Stanley was the obvious choice as he had been on the estate the longest.

When Stanley was interviewed by Mr Howard he told him he had been on the estate since 1936. 'Good Lord', said Mr Howard, 'and I hardly know you'. The truth was that he had never even spoken to Stanley before. In fact he hardly ever spoke to anyone on a shoot day and, in Stanley's words, 'could be rather odd at times. He was a fairly good Shot with his

Purdeys and loader, but he was away from home a lot with his BBC commitments (a governor from 1972 and Chairman 1980–83) and everything to do with the shooting parties had to be organised for him by his wife, Lady Cecilia, the daughter of the Duke of Grafton. When he came home at the weekend all he had to do was pick up a gun.'

Stanley started on £12 a week in 1964, payable fortnightly in arrears, but there was also a dog allowance of 10s a week and the cottage was rent and rates free. He had the help of five other keepers as the idea was to build the shoot up; Mr Howard had started to take land back, at the same time injecting a considerable amount of cash. Thus bags rose from around 120 in 1964 to over 400, Stanley's highest being 700 for one day.

There has been a steady stream of interesting guests on the mostly two-day shoots. Lord Whitelaw has been a regular – 'a grand chap, not an outstanding Shot but he killed a hundred birds here one day and he was very pleased with that'.

But like all headkeepers, Stanley did not actually see much of the Guns on shoot days: he was too busy organising his retinue. 'Sometimes I did not see them at all until after the last drive. One of my biggest problems was getting 'em back out after lunch at the Castle. This usually went on from 1 to 2.30pm or 2.45pm and, of course, there wasn't much light left then in December – perhaps time for only one short drive. And you hadn't to strike a match when you passed those merry Guns! It was entirely Lord Howard's fault.'

Yet Stanley obviously had great respect for his master. 'Lord Howard once shot a pheasant which fell through the ice on a pond near the house. A keeper's spaniel was sent to retrieve it, but fell through and couldn't get out . Without hesitation, Lord Howard plunged into the icy water up to his neck, with stick in hand to smash his way through to the struggling dog.

'Eventually he succeeded and the dog scrambled out, but it took about seven of us to free Lord Howard as it was very muddy and he was a very big chap.

'It was a wonderful effort on his behalf and I decided to write to the RSPCA about it as I thought they should give him one of their awards. But do you know they threw it out because it happened on a shoot day, despite the fact it certainly saved the dog's life. I was furious, and when I told her ladyship about it she said: "Well, I've patronised the RSPCA for years, but I'm afraid this will have to be the end of it."'

Lady Cecilia was involved in another shooting incident which remains clear in Stanley's mind, though she never used a gun herself. 'We were driving partridges, hares and rabbits with the tenant farmers and there were three Guns each side of a fence when we came to a potentially dangerous spot where I had placed a blue plastic bag in the fence, to warn people not to shoot towards it.

'At the end of the drive a hare came forward and one of the Guns swung through it and towards the bag. I cried out "No, No", but he still fired and immediately there was a yell from the other side. The silly … had put a few pellets into the legs of both another Gun and her ladyship, who was standing with him.

'We used to have up to fifty volunteers on hare shoots as the agent used to write to the tenant farmers saying "Bring a friend". I never knew who would turn up and many of them would be very inexperienced.'

Another guest from the world of television was one-time BBC director-general Alisdair Milne, who certainly made an impression on Stanley, but for all the wrong reasons. 'Judging by what he left me at night, I don't think he was a shooting man: he never left me a penny!'

The 'undesirables' also included the then boss of the Comet

discount shops, Mr Hollingbury. 'His syndicate bought five days one year and eight the next and he complained about everything. On his last day we guaranteed a bag of 200 and they shot 232, yet he still moaned to me. When I told Lord Howard he said: "Right, he's out". Mind you, Hollingbury didn't winge when we shot 400!'

Stanley retired from full-time keepering in 1983, but did a further three years part-time. He received his CLA long-service award for forty-seven years in 1988, and now lives in a delightful divided cottage on the estate, where he and his wife tend a very traditional garden bursting with flowers and magnificent vegetables. But he stresses that 'the pheasant is not the gardener's friend', and he now views them differently as they parade along his wall.

Typically Spartan, but interesting with its mementoes of old country life, the Ware cottage is extremely quiet – when I was there the only sounds were the tick of the clock and, appropriately, the occasional *kok-kok* of a pheasant. It is indeed a fitting place in which to recall the highlights of a successful partnership. For Mrs Ware there is the cherished memory of being given a small role, along with other locals, when Paul Newman, Sophia Loren and David Niven came to film at Castle Howard; and for Stanley there is immense pride in a lifetime devoted to sporting duty, throughout which 'everyone called me Stan – even his lordship'.

ROUGH AND READY

---- ○○○○○ ----

Being one of nine children in a struggling working-class family just after World War I, Frederick Ernest Ladhams had no easy upbringing. 'It was certainly rough and ready and the weak 'uns went to the wall.' But at least his tough childhood near London gave him the mental armour to cope with the rogues he would meet in later life.

The son of a foundry worker and grandson of a building labourer, Fred was born in a rented house on 31 January 1913, at Epping in Essex. 'There were no bathrooms then and father used to come home filthy, strip off to waist and wash outside with water boiled over an open fire. I can still smell the carbolic soap.

'Now an insurance company's office stands on the site of our old house, but then it was all fields round about and I was always interested in the country.

'Our old headmaster at Epping Boys School used to let keeper Robin Taylor take about twelve to twenty of us beating at Copped Hall on a school day. There was no fixed age – all you had to be was big and strong enough. We got half-a-crown, a bottle of pop and two sandwiches – one saltbeef, the other cheese – which you could hardly get in your mouth.'

But although he allowed the boys to go off beating, the head-master was, like most of his contemporaries, 'a real disciplinarian. You were caned for fighting and even if you was heard cheekin' someone in the town. Also, whenever the infants messed themselves, because they wasn't properly house-trained, us older ones had to take 'em out and clean 'em up. But the head and two masters lived at the school, where there was good gardens and we learned how to grow things and prune trees.'

Fred had several ways of earning pocket money. 'In those days there were lots of horses in London and I used to help uncle take hay and bedding down to them. When I was a bit older I was allowed to drive a second horse and cart down behind him. And on a Sunday I sometimes used to go down the local golf course to carry the clubs and get a bob or two.

'Also there used to be lots of wild flowers about Epping then. There was white and purple violets, peggles [cowslips], prim-roses and bluebells and we used to go and get 'em without the keeper seeing us. Then on a Sunday we used to sit out on the green and sell them to the cyclists for 3d a bunch. There were lots of cycling clubs out of London then.'

In addition, Fred had the customary schoolboy's paper round, for which he earned 1/6d a week.

But there was also plenty of wildlife to interest a budding young countryman in Epping between the wars. 'Lots of fallow deer, of course, and always plenty of badgers and birds' nests to find. And all of us boys and girls used to bathe together in a local pond. We took down a bar of soap and 'ad great fun. In them days you had to make your own entertainment.'

On leaving school at the age of fourteen, Fred replaced his older brother as boy keeper at Copped Hall, then owned by the 'very autocratic Mr Whyse and later bought by pop star Rod Stewart. There was a massive staff then, including two chauf-feurs for two Rolls Royces, three people in the laundry alone, and even an old lady who made butter.

'The butter lady was given one cock pheasant each year. When I took it up to her she always put a shilling on the table in front of me, along with half a glass of port – good stuff that was. Each farm worker had an annual brace of rabbits but tenant farmers and local police had a brace of pheasants each.

'I was allowed to pick myself out two rabbits each week and at Christmas I always got a ticket from the squire for so much beef. The last one I 'ad was worth about 7/6d. Then I got a couple of dozen eggs a week and we used to collect blackberries for the squire at 6d a pound. Altogether I got about £4 for the berries and a woman used to come down from the squire's London home in Nightingale Square to collect them for jam etc. She also took back chickens, cream and other fresh produce.

'My wage was ten shillings to start and after seven years I was on twenty-five shillings. I always gave money to Mum. I didn't get a suit of clothes till I'd been there three years.

'The headkeeper lived down in the Warren – a wood of big, old chestnut trees. I used to look after half his garden as well as the ferrets, chickens and dogs, including those Sealyham terriers for huntin' the wood out for rabbits. I even 'ad to clean the headkeeper's wife's brasses.

'Two or three days before a shoot I'd get a big bit of beef and cook it in a big, black pot in the copper house. This was for the beaters' sandwiches, each lot being wrapped in greaseproof paper. There was also coffee provided, and five-gallon casks of Whitbread beer. The Guns always went to the shooting box and the butler and maid brought out their lunch from the hall.'

Poaching was a considerable problem on London's doorstep. 'They was mostly after rabbits with snares, but we never stood any nonsense. Even if we walked on someone pickin' blackberries we tipped their basket upside down. You 'ad to be tough then and nip things in the bud. I even used to go down to some ivy trees, where birds was vulnerable, to drive pheasants out from roost so nobody could creep in and shoot them.'

In those days partridges were still common around Epping. 'One time in September, Mr Dashwood, the agent, and three

Guns, with us four keepers and the gardener beatin', shot fifty brace of partridges. It was mostly English birds then and they were all wild. The cropping just suited 'em perfectly. You got your roots and you got your arable, with plenty of stubble left too.'

Another of Fred's sidelines at Copped Hall was, 'rearing about six litters of ferrets in the summer. We used to advertise them at ten bob each in the *Exchange and Mart* and I got a shilling for each one sold. We got enquiries from all over and often sent 'em to southern Ireland. The Irish stamps always came upside down on the envelopes. People used to say it was a deliberate insult to the Crown.'

At the age of twenty-one, in the spring of 1935, Fred left home for the first time, to become one of three underkeepers at Sir Fred Jones's Irnham Hall, near Bourne in Lincolnshire. 'I only earned thirty-five shillings a week and paid £1 for lodging with the cowman, but meals was included. Iris joined me in 1936, when we were married; the gate lodge where we stayed was like a little castle.' However, Fred was able to add significantly to his income through rabbiting, being paid 6d a couple for those caught. 'Sir Fred was eighty then and his chauffeur actually had to hold him under the arms while he shot. He died after I was there a year and then his son Walter took over.'

'On a Saturday I used to pick up as many as 200 pheasant and partridge eggs along the roadsides. It was all arable there and they had tractors when everyone else was still using horses.

'Once the miners came out to plant a wood. The Government fetched 'em down in camps. When they came they was as thin and pale as that heater in the corner, but when they went back they was as tanned and healthy as anythin'.

'It was at Bulby Wood, which was supposed to be haunted, that I had the first instance of foxes being turned in on me [brought from another area and released] – for the hunt. There were three let go, but I shot 'em easily next morning as they were very tame. I'd seen their tracks in a sandbar along the beck. Later on they did the same to me in Oxfordshire, with a lot of big 'uns, but I nailed 'em all right. No way were we going to have foxes on the beat, hunt or no hunt!'

In 1937, at the age of twenty-three, Fred became underkeeper for Colonel Clifton at Clifton Hall, just south of Nottingham. 'We had to go to Beeston to be measured up for our suits – real Robin Hood jobs in Lincoln green.

'It was an awful place for poachers. They even used to creep round our bungalow at night to see if we were there talking.

'One night on roost watch this motorbike and sidecar went by us and later on, after we'd been home, we looked up and saw three fellows stickin' out like turkeys in the moonlight. We went up the wood to head them off, but there was not a twig cracklin' or bird twitterin', so we went round the other end and then ran straight into 'em.

'The old one kept comin' in and comin' in. Then I left off to set after the others. When I caught them we 'ad a good set-to and they threatened to shoot me, so I went back to help the head with the old boy. He still kept comin', but eventually the head 'it 'im with a stick and cut his face right open. Then we spun 'im round and got the cuffs on.

'Then we went back and got the car and chauffeur to take 'im down to Shire Hall at Nottingham. When we got him in the light there was blood all over the place and the sergeant said, "What the hell you been doin' with 'im?" He was a real poacher. His case came up just before Christmas and he got three months. We found out 'e was fifty-nine and he 'ad convictions goin' back to when he was a boy in 1890 – for everything from fowl stealing to pheasant poaching. His mates were in the court watchin' but we couldn't prove anything and they got away with it.'

Occasionally it was the keepers who came off worse. 'Once Johnny was cut right down the face by a longnetter's stick with a spike on the end. It really was a bad place and you 'ad to be watchin' all the time. As far as the birds was concerned, we always used to say that if you don't sleep with 'em you don't get 'em!

'Another time we were out in the moonlight when we heard thirty-six shots on nearby Thrumpton, the small place which Lord Byron used to own. Next day we went to see the keeper there and he said he'd been out and never got 'em. He claimed 'e challenged 'em and they dropped a bag with thirty-six pheasants in. But I said to Johnny Thomas, the headkeeper, "I reckon he stood off a bit because 'e was too scared".'

But at least the endless hours of nightwatching sometimes

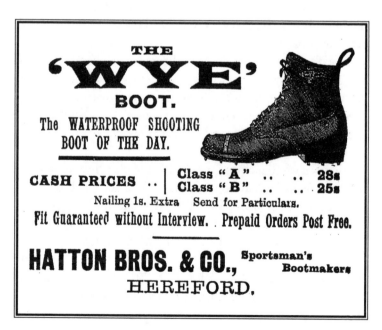

brought Fred light relief. 'Once I was walkin' home in the bright moonlight and spotted this ol' bull-nosed Morris just turned off the road. There was a couple inside havin' a right old go – at 2am!'

While courting couples have entertained many a keeper, few have had such a surprise as that which lay in store for Fred when blanking-in Clifton Wood one day. 'We were goin' along nicely when one of the chaps called out, "'ey up Fred, there's a lass lays 'ere". So I went over and there she was, half under a bush. Her hair was perfect, but when we turned her over her face was half gone with maggots.

'The lads said, "What's to do Fred", so I said we'd carry on and beat the wood out as she wasn't goin' anywhere. Then after the drive I 'ad a conflab with the boss and he said we'd finish the shoot. When we got back we told the police but it was 10pm that night before the sergeant and a constable came knockin' on the door. Then we got the tractor and took 'em down. The sergeant poked about under 'er and found some bottles and a note. "Oh, it's a suicide", he said, "we don't bother much about those." Anyway, we got her on a hurdle to carry her to the tractor. But what a stink! I made sure I was upwind when we took her up. A few weeks later I discovered that her fiancé had died suddenly – very sad.'

Fred had another encounter with tragedy at Clifton. 'We were goin' along the road lookin' for eggs when we came upon this old woman wringing her hands. She told us that her husband was missing and asked if we would help look around for him.

'Nearby was a stackyard with a well in the middle and I noticed a stick was on it. I said, "I bet he's in there", and sure enough 'e was – floatin' face down! He'd drowned himself and we found out later that they were going to put 'im in the infirmary, but he didn't want to go.'

Not surprisingly, Fred was keen to move on to pastures new,

to gain valuable experience, so he advertised and in 1939 was offered a partridge beat at Blenheim.

'Headkeeper Mr Grey was no worker, more of a gentleman who just rode around on a BSA 250 motorbike makin' sure everythin' was all right. And there was another chap who did nothing but fetch the feed for us keepers with his pony and trap.'

At that time Blenheim's agriculture was well suited to partridge production, providing plenty of natural food. 'We used to fetch the eggs for 'em from the ant 'eaps in the fields. When the sun was out the ants brought the eggs to the surface and then we took a spade to 'em and popped 'em in a bucket – just like slicing off a molehill. Baby partridges thrive on ant eggs, but you mustn't give 'em too many as they like 'em so much they might then refuse anything else. Blenheim was the only place I've been where we could do this. The 'eaps were on the rough grazing and Iris used to help me with them.

'Nowadays people just moan about the disappearance of the partridge, but if you want them back you've simply got to buckle down and look after 'em. Also you've got to strip every pheasant egg off a partridge beat as the pheasant is just like a cuckoo and will lay in every nest.

'Our house was pretty primitive at Blenheim, with all oil lamps and water from the well. The track down to it was a rough old thing and Iris used to say it shook all the nuts off the pram.

'I earned two guineas a week at Blenheim and was given the feed for thirty hens, which kept us in eggs. My leggings was brown leather, whereas they were boxcloth back in Lincolnshire. And I had a black bowler which I was supposed to wear all the time, but whenever I could I only wore it on shoot days because you looked a real case in it.

'They was very strict then and you only spoke to the duke when you was spoken to. Your hat 'ad to come off pretty smart and you didn't 'ave to 'ave a fag on your lip. Nowadays they get away with murder. But at the same time a keeper was really somethin' in the community then.'

Notwithstanding the strictness of the regime, Fred soon settled in and produced the required results. 'When they shot my beat in September 1939 they got 100 brace and ninety per cent were young. Actually the Guns killed ninety-five brace so the headkeeper told me to take some cartridges and go out in the morning to get another ten birds so that it would look better in the gamebook. Nobody knew any different.'

There was some superb shooting at Blenheim during Fred's time. 'With two lines of beaters there was never any hanging about. There were only four big-bang drives – two in the morning and two in the afternoon. Combe Bottom was fantastic – no bang-bang and then a space like at most places. The birds came out like clouds of starlings and in 1939 they shot 400 on just that one drive when there was 1,500 pheasants for the day. I think it must have been some sort of record at the time because I remember there was a fair bit of jealousy with Lord Derby's Knowsley Hall. But there were some crack Shots to get the bags. The then duchess was one of the best I've seen. It was all double guns.'

The duke too was a keen Shot. 'Even if anyone missed on his family day, when they went round in an old bus, he used to shout at 'em, "If you can't hit them you might as well go home". He was a great big feller who used to march straight through the irrigation channels followed by his very short loader carrying his gun over his head. It was very comical. And there was a model railway at the palace which was supposed to be for the young marquis, but the duke spent most of his time on it.'

'Later on they tried to get us Blenheim keepers to form a special brigade of territorials, but in the end, with the war, all rearing stopped and in spring 1940 everyone of service age had to leave. So then Iris and me went back to Essex and I had just odd jobs – mostly building tank traps – before I was called up.'

In due course, Fred was summoned to Walthamstow for a medical and was 'pronounced A1, but they always gave you the opposite of what you wanted to do. Three weeks later I was called up to Exeter and then posted to Blandford, Dorset, as part of the Royal Artillery Searchlight Regiment – 546 Battery.'

In 1941 Fred was posted to Northern Ireland, 'to Dunoon in the Antrim Hills around Belfast, where there were miles of heather and I saw my first grouse as well as lots of brown trout in the tarns. We stayed there till the summer of '43, but there was not much doin'. I never saw a single keeper when I was goin' around the woods and most of the lads with me there came out of London and had never even seen a tree let alone a pheasant. But one good thing over there was that they would give you anything as long as you 'ad the money to pay for it. There was never any worry about coupons.'

After further postings at home and abroad, Fred then decided that he was too old for the infantry although he was only thirty-one, and 'wangled it to go in the cookhouse', eventually leaving the Army as a private in 1946, without any regrets. 'I tell you what – England's the place to be. When we were on the boat comin' home there was an announcement saying, "Anyone want to see the white cliffs of Dover?" Well, it's a wonder the boat didn't turn turtle there was such a rush to one side.'

The war years had been far from pleasant for Iris too. To begin with, when the Ladhams moved from Blenheim to London the pipes in their house froze, eventually bursting and causing such damp their first son died of pneumonia at only two years old. And when Fred was abroad Iris had a telegram to say he was missing. 'But it turned out he had a touch of malaria and was in hospital, where they mixed him up with another chap. And they never paid me any pension while he was missing!'

When Fred left the Army he had accrued ten weeks' paid leave. 'I was free as a bird and I took every day of it. But I always intended to go back to keepering. I wrote to Blenheim and Nottingham, but it was dead there so I asked keeper Johnny Thomas to advertise for me. I ended up going to Lowther, near Penrith, in July 1946, under headkeeper William Semple, and remained there till I retired.

'Viscount Lowther was a bit autocratic – just like it was before the war. He used to ride around on a big, white horse and every Sunday for a few weeks before the season opened he'd get the keepers out and walk in line with us just to see what the grouse was like. He was a very keen Shot and hated shooting any gamebird up the arse. He died of cancer at fifty-nine.

'There were some real characters about then. One old farmer

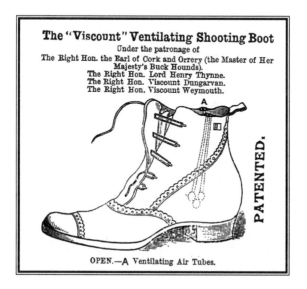

The "Viscount" Ventilating Shooting Boot

Under the patronage of
The Right Hon. the Earl of Cork and Orrery (the Master of Her Majesty's Buck Hounds).
The Right Hon. Lord Henry Thynne.
The Right Hon. Viscount Dungarvan.
The Right Hon. Viscount Weymouth.

PATENTED.

OPEN.—A Ventilating Air Tubes.

– Isaac Cookson from Sceough Fell – used to cut the bracken for cattle bedding using a long-handled corn scythe and bring it down with a sledge drawn by a Galloway pony. He also took the ling for his fire. His long, white beard was tucked into his belt, and when he took his home-made butter to Penrith market people was scared to sit beside him on the bus.'

Fred's first beat at Lowther was Buck Holme Woods, but later he had others. 'And the 6,000 to 7,000-acre Helton beat, between Ullswater and Haweswater, had it all, with red deer, roe deer, blackgame and partridges as well as grouse and pheasants.

'The whole estate was about 70,000 acres and some 50,000 was shot. One season we 'ad forty shoot days on grouse and pheasants and none was reared. Also only cock pheasants was shot because the Viscount said it was best to leave the hens. When I had Buck Holme we once shot 119 cocks. Well, it was 120 with one hen – a very dark bird, bagged by Chief Constable Brown of Cumbria, but he did apologise for his mistake.'

When Fred arrived at Lowther he joined an ageing team. 'I was one of the first new blood. We were paid on the first Monday of the month and when I went up for it I was like a baby compared to all the others. Before that I'd been paid fortnightly. My wages was £3 5s plus 2s a day shoot lunch money, 1s a week each for keeping two ferrets, 3/6d a week each for two retrievers and 1/6d a week for a terrier. The dog and lunch money was paid every six months and they made you sign in a book for it. The secretary was old John Peel – a descendant of the real one.

'Viscount Lowther ran the estate for the sixth Earl – Lance, and when he died the grandson James took over very young as the seventh Earl. So then I worked for the Hon Captain Lowther. It stayed entirely a private shoot till 1949 and we used to shoot for six days solid from the 12th. The third year I was there we killed 168 brace on Shap.

'I used to load for Viscount Lowther and 'e was a strict ol' boy in the butt. One day 'e asked me whether it was thirteen or fourteen grouse he 'ad down and I said I wasn't quite sure. He said, "You should bloody well know – that's why you're here". But next time round he asked for me again, so I couldn't have done that badly.'

During Fred's time at Lowther the estate held coursing meetings. 'We used to go round to the other estates and net hares to bring in. There was never too much trouble with poachers as once a year Captain Lowther used to give the gypsies – about forty to fifty of 'em – a Sunday runnin' greyhounds at hares on Askham Fell. Shocker Bowman used to get 'em all together and they would bet against each other. That kept 'em happy for a twelve month. The seventh Earl stopped all that.

'But there used to be quite a bit of trouble with salmon poachers on the river. So one day in my second year we were joined by three water board fellers and I got another young chap to help. We saw a light comin' down to the swing bridge and there were some men either side of the river. We were in a hollow and you could 'ave 'eard 'em comin' at Penrith they made so much noise.

'Then suddenly they were there, looking huge on the skyline above. One chap 'ad a gaff and two salmon over his shoulder, so I went for 'im and grabbed him round the waist. But my mate Brodie jumped on top of me and the others didn't come in, so we only got the one. It cost 'im sixteen guineas, but 'e said, "Will you take a cheque?" The fine was nothin' to 'im. He made hundreds out of salmon durin' the war, and they were great big fish then. Still, it was hell of a shock to 'em as they'd been gettin' away with it for years, and things quietened down a bit after that.'

Sometimes Fred also had to take people stalking. 'One chap

was so excited at shooting a royal 'e left 'is glasses on the spot. But when he told me it was too dark to do anythin' about it. So next morning I took a couple of others up there to search for 'em. Well, we were just walking up the moor in line when I saw the glasses glinting in the sunlight. He were a lucky chap.

'We also used to take the occasional two-year-old pricket stag in and fatten it up for the castle – just like raisin' a steer.'

Like so many keepers, Fred first had a motorbike for transport. 'It was a BSA 125 which ran on Petroil and you could take it anywhere.' Then he had a Bond three-wheeler car, 'which you 'ad to kick-start on a cold morning because the battery was hopeless.'

Later on, Captain Lowther's Whitbysteads syndicate bought Fred a new, M-registration Robin Reliant, the 3-wheeler being popular because it could be driven with only a motorcycle licence. 'I had that for four years and then they bought me another new one for £900, and fourteen years ago a third for £3,000. I still had the Robin when I retired and did not give it up until 1990. I even used to take it out on the grouse moor, but the only trouble was in snow, when you couldn't follow the tracks of the other vehicles.'

The worst winter that Fred could remember was that of 1946–7. 'It was the July before all the snow went at Haweswater and our house was completely cut off for three weeks. You could only just see the tops of some of the telegraph poles and our only fuel was some dead oak trees which we cut down. We were down to our last cup of flour before they dug us out. Then just after I managed to get out for some supplies the wind got up and blew the snow back in again. It was no good shootin' a rabbit as they was all skin and bone. And thousands of sheep were wiped out on the fells, but it was a good year for carrion crows with all the dead meat to feed off.'

But despite all the hardships, Fred Ladhams 'would do it all again. After all, there were plenty of good times. And I've been all over with the bosses loadin' – it was just like bein' on holiday with your keep found.'

Fred retired in 1978, but did a further two years part-time for the Lowther estate. He and Iris are still close to the Cumbrian countryside, in the small market town of Kirkby Stephen.

BOULTON AND PAUL,
NORWICH.
PORTABLE DOG KENNELS.

These kennels are well made and highly finished. All parts are accessible for cleansing and disinfecting. The entrance being at the side, with an inside partition, affords a warm and dry bed in all weathers. They take to pieces and pack flat for travelling.

CASH PRICES, CARRIAGE PAID.

For Terriers.................................. .... 1 5 0
For Collies, Spaniels, or Retrievers ... 2 2 0
For St. Bernards or Mastiffs............ 3 3 0

Orders executed on receipt.

Every requisite for the Kennel, Poultry Yard Pheasantry, Aviary, &c., manufactured by ourselves.

CATALOGUE FREE BY POST.

ON THE EDGE
OF PARADISE

———————— ooooo ————————

It was entirely appropriate that Donald Ford arrived in this world on the edge of a place called Paradise Wood, for he found life there almost idyllic. Born just three days before Christmas 1926, at Stourpaine, near Blandford in Dorset, he revelled in the unspoilt countryside. But perhaps that is not so surprising considering the fact his father, grandfather, great-grandfather and great-great-grandfather were all keepers before him, on Lord Portman's estate.

Don was out with his father from the word go, helping with tasks such as setting gins, almost before he could walk. 'I used to traipse miles with father around his tunnel traps even before I went to school at the age of five. It was a wonderful place, with skylarks everywhere going up and down, and on the land it was all horses, with lots of downland, ploughin', drillin' and har-rowin'. Dog roses and fruits covered the hedges, which were all overgrown – ideal for game but a nightmare for vermin control. We used to hang up stoats and everything else on a gibbet so that the boss could see the keeper was doin' his job. They made an awful smell. Everywhere you went there was a terrific lot of skeletons on the bushes, from a weasel to a black-backed gull.

'At night I helped father make snares, using a piece of wood with two nails and wire bought by the pound. Six-strand wire was OK for most work, but on hills 8lb was necessary because the rabbits runnin' down would thump it so hard. To braid it we put the wire through a meat skewer and then through the handle of a flat iron, which was given a good twist.

'We ran up to 300 snares and they had to be just right. Night-time I went with father to hold the torch, but sometimes Mum wouldn't allow it when there was school next day. I also ran my own little line of twelve or fifteen snares, which I went to in the morning before going to school. A taxi used to fetch us at eight because we were isolated, over five miles from Wareham.'

Don also helped with shooting many hundreds of rabbits. 'I had my first shot. with a .410, when I was four. I remember it well because it was a Sunday, when Mum never worked because she was the daughter of a Methodist preacher and quite religious. We were on the lawn and father stood an apricot can on a post. He put just one 2in cartridge in the side-by-side hammergun, pulled the hammer back and passed me the gun. Off it went and the first thing I did was run over and see how many holes were in the tin. Years later, I did the same thing with my sons and grandson at four years old.

'When I was about ten I used to crawl miles with that .410, peepin' over banks after rabbits. And sometimes I'd walk up and jump out so that I could shoot 'em runnin'. I shot my first runner when I was seven.

'We used to poke sheets of paper soaked with Renardine down the rabbit holes for a couple of days and that made the rabbits sit out in the bushes. Then a shoot day would be a hell of a session. It was always a Saturday as that meant some of the farmworkers could come too. One time I shot my first woodcock, and my arm was black and blue because I shot all day, but I wouldn't say it was too long. I must have fired 100 and some odd cartridges that day. All this made up my mind that keepering would be the life for me.'

Don certainly had plenty of opportunity to check that he was truly suited to the life. When he was twelve, his father was bedridden with sciatica and Don had to take over for a fortnight. 'We still had some of the old coops and it was very hard work, but I enjoyed it. You had to be very careful with mixing the food. If there was too much and some was left and the sun got on it then the birds soon got scour. After the fortnight Father was really pleased.'

When the family was at Winterborne Tomson, Don went to Almer School (now a keeper's house), near Blandford, where his father was a single-handed keeper. 'From there we moved to Arne, near Wareham, where Dad was head. When I was fourteen, the family moved to Kingston, near Corfe Castle, and I went as trainee on the Encombe estate, where Father was head.'

When he was seventeen, Don volunteered for the Army, 'because they brought in the Bevan boys and I didn't want to go down the mines. Luckily, they didn't query my age, not being eighteen. I trained for six weeks at Colchester, then Norfolk, where I reckon I walked the whole of the county practising to be an infantryman in the Dorset Regiment. And I was very soon picked out for rifle shooting. The sergeant said, "You shoot some of those bloody Germans who shot my brother".' But Don never had the opportunity. Although he was posted to Gibraltar and Berlin, he was still in training on VE Day.

However, Don did have plenty of opportunity for sporting shooting during the war years. 'I always remember the night they bombed Coventry. I'd shot an Army haversackful of teal and on the way home was dodgin' the shrapnel. You could see all the planes as clear as anythin' in the moonlight.'

Fortunately, the family came through the war unscathed. 'The house we had been in at Arne was bombed and flattened, along with the kennels, because they had the ack-ack guns there. Another keeper lived there at the time, but luckily he wasn't in when Gerry called.'

After the war it was back to Encombe for two years. Then Don worked for three years as a beatkeeper for Major David Wills, on the Lichfield Manor estate, near Newbury. This was followed by eighteen months on Sir Anthony Tichborne's estate, near Alresford, Hampshire. At the age of twenty-six he went to Sussex, to run a syndicate for Jack Aylwood, who took over from Sir Tom Sopwith. Don really enjoyed it there, but decided to leave in 1974 after twenty-two years when Aylwood died of cancer. He went to Lord Shaftesbury's Dorset estate at picturesque Wimborne St Giles, retiring as headkeeper at the age of sixty-five after seeing the 1991–2 season through. He is one of the few lucky keepers in recent years who have been given retirement homes on the estates they have served.

Much of Don's life has been spent controlling predators of game ('vermin'), but in the old days he was allowed to use poisons as well as a whole arsenal of vicious traps. 'Strychnine was the best, especially in a half-buried rabbit for foxes. Then there was arsenic and, later on, zinc phosphide and Rodine for rats. We used to get a rabbit, slit it open and put Rodine on the liver – this was deadly for crows, which also came to the egg tray, a shelf 7–8ft up against a tree. Owls and other birds of prey were taken in pole traps. It's all illegal now, of course, which makes keeperin' so much harder.

'I caught my first fox at the age of twelve, to a pig which I found buried in a clump of trees, in a 6in grave. The foxes had already been there and eaten into it, so it was all smelly and falling to pieces. So I put some traps there, the big 6in badger gins. Later I went back, but there was nothing there. I told Dad and when he went there was a lovely fox with a white tip to its tail. I was really disappointed that I was the one to catch it but not kill it.

'Sometimes we used to half-bury a cat on a mound which

foxes liked to roll on and do their business. One place I had six traps and the first night I caught a vixen, which I skinned there and then, rolled the carcass on top of the mound and part covered it. Then I had nine more foxes in eleven days. When I was watchin' and could see the round shape of the mound I knew all was OK, but when I saw Charlie's silhouette dancin' around it was straight out with the gun.

'You can't beat a few spots of hare blood around your tunnel traps – brilliant! Then, if there's a stoat or weasel in the area you've got it. If you catch a rat or a stoat and get a bit of blood on the trap pan, next mornin' you always catch again. That's because they think it's been used by another and it's OK.'

But what Don regards as the most destructive of all predators is relatively new to the British countryside, having escaped from fur farms to establish feral populations in most areas. 'The mink is the worst vermin of all. It can swim, jump, run and climb and has no enemy here except the human.

'The first time I had trouble with mink was back in 1964, when I had three dozen point-of-lay pullets in a pen. One morning I went to feed them and there was blood all over the snow and two or three birds dead in the pen. I dashed in the hut and there was a big pile of dead pullets, some with their heads off, and one or two barely alive. Immediately I thought it was the work of a ferret, grabbed an armful of traps and went to put one by a hole. But then I saw whiskers – he was still in there! So I went back and got the gun, gave a squeak, out came his head, and bang! He was really big – I couldn't get my hand round his neck. And the smell!

'Then I thought I'd get lots of money for the skin and sent it up to Horace Friend. But he said it was useless as it was wild and I got nothing. However, in later years they started taking 'em and I got up to £3 a skin.

'The mink will do no end of damage in the release pen. Once in Sussex I picked up 109 nine-week-old poults killed by one animal. You could tell it was a mink by the two little needle marks on top of the head. This devil only ate one bird, leaving the wings, head and gizzard, but some were part buried. Anyway, I already had twenty-two tunnel traps in the area, so I put more traps all over the place, some in tree stumps baited with turkey innards I got from Petersfield. But the mink didn't come for three nights. Then he climbed in, killed more birds and dug his way out. After that he left off for ten days and didn't go to any of the baits or tunnel traps. Sometimes after he'd been there were birds part live and next morning. He used to kill birds which were roosting up in the old man's beard and I never did catch him.'

One of Don's most unexpected catches was two badger cubs trapped by their feet in a gin. 'I took them home, put Vaseline on their feet and reared them in a shed with turf on the concrete floor. Later I sold them to Ferndown Zoological Gardens.'

Like so many keepers, Don has lost a lot of game to poachers as well as predators. 'Sundays have always been bad as the casual poachers go round the roads with their catapults and air rifles. And a lot of gyppos take hares and deer. Now there are night patrols all the time. This shoot would be nothing without that. Some of these gyppos knew this land way back when they grew mangolds here, so they know it even better than me. Now they live in council houses and even own their own homes. Some say they bought them on the proceeds of poachin', just to annoy you.'

Back in Sussex, Don used an age-old method to frighten off both poachers and foxes. But his were not any old scarecrows. Indeed, 'people used to say how well-dressed they were. The body was wire netting, the head a paper bag, and they wore rubber boots, a hat and an old suit. Each one carried a lantern –

a gallon petrol can with one side cut out, a 2lb jam jar inside with a night light top and a long wick. I filled it up weekly. The whole thing swivelled and flashed and the more you looked at it in the gloom the more you was convinced it was comin' towards you. We had them up every ride and they scared off lots of intruders.'

Once, however, it was Don who was surprised by a scarecrow. 'I was putting some birds to wood, and the night before I was getting the scarecrows ready. I was marchin' along with one under each arm when suddenly I felt something round the back of my neck. It was a dormouse which had its nest in the head of a dummy. Anyway, I caught it and put it in this old shepherd's hut where there was an old corn bin and I thought he couldn't get out. When I went back next day he was still there so I gave him some bits to make another nest. Then I took this ol' canary cage up to the wood and put 'im in it. I even went to Petersfield and bought 'im some nuts.

'Eventually I noticed that he was getting unusually fat and was astonished when four young ones appeared. But I reared 'em successfully. Then the Forestry Commission got to know of it and one of their men came all the way from Scotland to see me, as dormice were never known to breed in captivity. He wanted to buy 'em, but I said you can have the young but I'll keep the old one. Fred Courtier, of the Forestry Commission in the New Forest, was given the job of lookin' after them in a big aviary.

'Not long after I was trimmin' away in the wood, where I sometimes put bags in pop-holes. I noticed one of these bags 7ft up in a fork and when I climbed up there was a nest inside with a dormouse fast asleep. It turned out to be a male, so I thought, all right now, I'll put it with my female, which had then been with me for two years. So I did, but a few weeks later the male became thin and died. Then the female went thin, got watery eyes and she died too. I don't know why.'

Don also has some very special memories of mice during the record-breaking freeze of winter 1962–3. 'Whenever I snared and skinned foxes the mice was so hungry they'd come out and strip the carcass bare. They even ate the plastic off the tops of the shock absorber springs to get at and eat the grease in my new Ford Anglia estate.

'That winter the snow came on Boxing Day and lasted til 3 March in Sussex. We were cut off all that time because we lived a mile from the main road, and we couldn't even shoot till the end of January, when we had a keepers' and beaters' day and shot 300 cocks. I still managed a nine-mile feed round on foot every day. Although I kept making tracks in the snow they constantly filled up with new drifts.'

When it comes to organising a shoot day Don has been a grand master, leaving no detail to chance. He even makes sure that he faces his Land-Rover away from a drive, 'as I've seen birds go through the screens'. But although he grew up in the old school of keepering he never dwelt in the past. In recent years he has been as familiar with walkie-talkies, radio-tagging of game and the management of let days, as the old skills of mixing your own pheasant feed.

'But how would an employer spot a good beatkeeper among so many applicants nowadays?' I asked Don. 'Easy,' he replied. 'First thing, shake 'im by the hand. If it's smooth he's no good, but if it's rough then you know he's a good trapper.'

EVERYONE CALLED
ME 'FOXY'

〇〇〇〇〇

T he grandson of a poacher and son of a market-gardener, Frank ('Foxy') Hunt has keepered in seven counties, but, as his wife is quick to point out, 'we always left of our own accord and to better ourselves.'

Frank was born on 15 January 1908 at Collingham, near Newark, Nottinghamshire, and his only experience of shooting before leaving school came through protecting the wheat on his father's allotment. 'The sparrows played hell with it so my father gave me an old muzzle-loader to shoot 'em.'

At the age of fourteen he was taken on as keeper's boy by Squire Curtis of Langford Hall, near Newark, the man who made his money through making gunpowder. He was also offered a job on the estate of Curtis' brother, on Tresco in the Scilly Isles, but his father said he was too young to go. So he stayed at home to mix feed, snare and bait traps for the squire.

After a year he went as keeper's boy for the Earl of Kimberley at North Walsham, on the Norfolk coast near Great Yarmouth, where he lodged with headkeeper Dawling. There he was put in charge of the donkey cart to take all the traps round – each keeper had ten dozen gins to look after. And he also had to take Mrs Dawling into North Walsham to do her shopping. 'She really fed me up on them there Norfolk dumplin's.'

Frank was paid £1 a week, but out of that he had to hand over 18s for board and lodging. Even so, on 2s spending money he managed to run a motorbike – a BSA 249, which his father loaned him £39 to buy. 'I remember going to visit my grandfather at Sleaford on it: quite an adventure in those days, and when I arrived safely at the farm everybody turned out to cheer.

'I remember those days so clearly. It always seemed to be foggy and the nearby Happisburgh Lighthouse made a terrible din all night long. But it was a peaceful place, too, and it was a real pleasure to go motorcycling in those days.

NO HUMANE SPORTSMAN
Should be without the Patent "HAWK" BIRD KILLER. The instrument causes instant death to winged or wounded birds, is simple in construction, easily carried and certain in action. For full particulars apply to the "HAWK" Manufacturing Co., Hexham. Prices, nickelplated "HAWK" BIRD KILLER, 3s. 6d.; ditto, with nickelplated Chain, 4s. 6d. Forwarded per post on receipt of P.O.O. for 3s. 8d. or 4s. 8d.

'There was no industry in the area, though, and the only work was on the land. It was a hard life an' all. One day I met this poor old boy along the way and he said he'd walked five miles to do a day's thrashing, but when he arrived he got nothing because it was too wet to work and they were only paid by results.

'On shoot days I went about with the donkey cart gathering the shot game from places where the horse-drawn, main game cart was too heavy to go.'

After five years in Norfolk, Frank went to work for Major Forbes at North Rode, near Congleton, Cheshire. But it was rather strange how the vacancy arose, and all because at North Rode the mansion stood beside a big lake – the Guns would shoot pheasants up to lunchtime, and then turn their attention to the duck. But it was a long way round the lake so the single underkeeper had to row the Guns across the water to their shooting stations. Unfortunately, one day he tipped them all in and got the sack. So when Frank took his place he had to learn to become a good boatman too.

'In those days there was always someone knocking on the door trying to sell pheasant food, and the reps were always giving the keepers tickets to get them to visit their stands at Crufts. Lowes looked after us well, but Spratts always did us the best with a rare old meal – a knife and fork do, and they really pushed the boat out. The headkeepers always went to one side of the stand through a special entrance and were given whisky, while the underkeepers went round the other side and had to make do with beer.'

Crufts was the traditional clearing house for keepering jobs and it was well known that anyone standing near the Spratt's stand holding a white handkerchief or suchlike was waiting to be identified by a prospective employer.

It was while at North Rode that young Hunt started courting his future wife, Elizabeth ('Betty'), who worked in a cotton mill, wore clogs and shawl and had never been in the country in her life. Betty told me 'We met when we were on short time and with nothing else to do my friend and me decided to go for a walk into the country. We were really enjoying ourselves and got a nice bunch of bluebells in the wood when all of a sudden someone came up behind us. "What the hell are you doin' here?" he bellowed. "And you can drop those", he said, staring at the bluebells we clutched nervously. "I have a lot of wild pheasants laying eggs here and I don't want anyone stompin' about breakin' 'em".

'But we wouldn't drop our flowers and the keeper ran us out

ROYAL AGRICULTURAL HALL - LONDON

CRUFT'S

GREAT INTERNATIONAL DOG SHOW

WEDNESDAY
FEB.
9TH

THURSDAY
FEB.
10TH

THE GREATEST DOG SHOW the World has ever seen for

SPORTING DOGS

SPECIAL CLASSES RESERVED FOR GAMEKEEPERS

GAMEKEEPER'S ASSOCIATION hold their ANNUAL SHOW
FEBRUARY 9 and 10   ::   Entries close January 24th

Judge for Gamekeepers' Classes   Mr. S. J. LING

I must go to Crufts!

IT'S THE GAMEKEEPERS SHOW

THE DOGS WILL BE BENCHED AND FED BY SPRATT'S PATENT LTD.

ooooo

of the wood. Then just as we were leaving he called out "I tell you what, I'll let you keep the flowers if you go out with me tonight". So I did, and that was how Frank and me began our life together.'

So, with a wife to support, Frank began to look for a better job, and he certainly came up trumps when he went to work as underkeeper for the extrovert Madame Sauber at Salcey Forest, between Newport Pagnell and Northampton. On this mixed shoot there was just one other keeper – the head – and the Hunts settled down happily in the ex-gardener's bothy in the rose garden.

When he attended for interview, Frank was met by Madame Sauber's chauffeur at the railway station. After a while they came to some big white gates and the chauffeur told Frank to jump out and open them. 'But when I did so he just whizzed past and left me standing, wondering what on earth was going on. Anyway, I followed him up the drive and eventually saw a lady sitting by some French windows. As soon as she saw me she let two awful terriers go at me. Trying to stay calm and stifle my anxiety, I put out my hand to the dogs and said, hopefully, "good boys". To my complete amazement and utter relief, they started wagging their tails.

'Then a high-pitched voice called out "Consider yourself engaged". The butler appeared like a statue by the kitchen door and declared "This way, please". He had a beautiful lunch waiting for me and while I was tucking in he started to interview me a bit. I even had a whole bottle of wine all to myself.

'Eventually, a bell rang, and the butler said "Madame will see you now". When I was ushered in, the first thing she said to me was "I expect you wondered why I said you were engaged when I hadn't even spoken to you. Well, I always engage my servants with those two dogs – John and Grouse. They always know an honest person – if they had bitten you I would have sent you back immediately".

'Then she asked me what money I wanted, so diplomatically I replied that she might care to suggest the amount. "All right, thirty shillings", she declared. "You will receive all your coal free and my head gardener will come round to your wife every morning to take her order for vegetables and fruit. A keeper hasn't the time to dig a garden." Thus began two years during which it seemed we couldn't do any wrong.

'Madame's husband was a German artist and their main house was in Knightsbridge. But they were both with us to shoot once a fortnight. She took such a liking to us she even left John and Grouse with us while she went to her villa in Monte Carlo. It was a great honour to be trusted so, but those dogs had to be really well looked after. They had a special cot each by our bed and every night we had to tuck them in with only their heads showing – just like babies. All the kennels were centrally heated and the butcher called every day to collect the kennelman's order.

'When she was home Madame used to send her lady's maid

round to ask Mrs Hunt if she would like to go to the opera in Northampton. And we never refused anything in case we were never asked again. I was never invited on one of these jaunts, only Betty, but she loved them. However, we did go to local dances together. It was great fun rolling up to a sixpenny hop in a Rolls Royce!

'For my work they gave me a huge Harley-Davidson motorbike and sidecar as well as a Ford car for our own use.

'On a shoot day the Guns came by train and we met them at the station. Everyone was extremely well looked after and there was even a special place for the dogs at lunch. Of course, with Madame's influence there were gallons and gallons of wine, and there was a great deal of whisky too. The bottles used to be stored in the coal shed after a weekend shoot and more than once I said "Bring the jug" as there was quite a bit left in some of the bottles.

'Talking about drink, I remember one day most distinctly. Madame had asked me to put a coop of pheasants on the lawn in front of the house so that she could enjoy watching the birds pecking about. But that night when I went to shut them up, I found her husband laid out on the lawn. When I went to pick him up she called out gruffly: "Leave him there or you'll be out." They had obviously been drinking heavily and he was blind drunk. However, later on she came and asked me to get him into the car as he had hit his head on the steps and needed medical attention.'

Life with Madame ended when Mrs Hunt became pregnant. There was 'no place for children there' and Frank was asked to consider looking for another position. Frank soon secured a job as one of five beatkeepers on Lord Hylton's 15,000-acre (6,070ha) Ammerdown Park estate between Radstock and Frome.

Lord Hylton had lost most of his interest in the shoot

through a great personal tragedy. He always had a snooze in the afternoon and one day when he was sound asleep his son Toby took the gun cabinet keys from his pocket. The lad removed a shotgun and went off rabbit shooting with his sister; when they were passing the gun through a hedge it went off and Toby was killed outright.

After that the shoot was taken up by a wealthy syndicate which included the tobacco family Wills and the jam-makers Robertson. But they had not been brought up to shoot in the tradition of landed gentry and needed to have coaching by Gibbs the gunmaker of Bristol. And as their enthusiasm increased, the keepers were required to rear more and more pheasants. Eventually Frank became headkeeper.

'Each beat was expected to provide a day's shooting, and lunch was always held at the headkeeper's cottage. The butler would come down and when all the Guns had taken their fill we used to entice them into the sitting room as quickly as possible, by lighting the fire to make them nice and cosy, so that we could move in and feast on the left-overs!

'About thirty local boys were employed as stops and they would all light fires to help keep the pheasants in. This also helped them to keep warm. They were all miners' sons and brought bags of coal along. Lunches were sent round to them along with jugs of hot cocoa, so they didn't go without. We had girls, too – and none of them seemed to mind the bitter winters we used to get.

'On the mantelpiece Betty kept a book and all the boys and girls used to come and enter their names in it, a couple of days before each shoot. Of course, they all wanted to earn a bit of pocket money and there was some competition among them. Sometimes they used to tease and suggest to each other that certain names were missing from the book. Then we would get irate fathers knocking on the door, wanting to know why young Johnny's name was not included.

'The children who did come received 2s 6d, a big lump of cheese, a pork pie and a bottle of pop, and the men beaters had 5s plus their lunch.

'Each beatkeeper was given five tons of coal a year, but, as headkeeper, I was given six even though I didn't need it. There was so much of it because it was produced on the estate and we never let our fires go out. When each new delivery came I gave what I had left over to the farmer up the road. We were supposed to pay the haulier but he never charged us. Anyway, we saw he was all right with a bird or two.

'My golly, didn't them ol' miners used to poach. We always had one down in the courts. They used to fight, too, but luckily I always seemed to come off best. And I joined up as a special constable to give me power over the roads. I was exempt from call-up because I was classified as a vermin destroyer.

'We had bombs dropped all over the estate when they missed Bristol. On one occasion her ladyship came out, complete with monocle, and said to me: "Weren't we lucky". But she didn't recognise me in my special's uniform directing the traffic. It was only when the shepherd accidentally let on that she twigged. And shortly afterwards his lordship marched up to me and said sharply: "I'll see you in the morning at 10am".

'Anyway, next day I duly reported to the office and his lordship said: "Do you get paid for that?" "Certainly not", I replied. And it was as well I didn't, as if I had he would certainly have cut my wages. But her ladyship was rather more sensitive and said to me: "My, you do look smart in your uniform, Mr Hunt".

'Of course, there was no rearing during the war with food rationed; then came one very sharp winter and I asked his lordship if I could buy a little corn for the birds. "Oh no", he said.

"Let them die: there's a war on, don't you know." But we weren't too badly off as I knew a friendly farmer up the road.

'I used to kill a few birds for the market and they should have been sold at the controlled price of 9s for cocks and 8s for hens, but if someone didn't give me £2 a brace then I wouldn't deal with them again. They didn't have any choice really as meat was in such short supply and everyone wanted it. They even went mad for rabbits.

'When his lordship died I was one of the chosen few to carry him to his grave in a horse-drawn farm waggon. The carter led the horse and four of us walked behind – me, the head gardener, the forester and the head carpenter, representing each department on the estate. The burial was at Kilminster, where his lordship used to pay the parson his living.

'Captain Jolliffe took over and I taught his two sons to shoot, just as I had already taught him. The syndicate was wound up and Captain Jolliffe took on all the shooting. His guests included Lord Bath, Major Duckworth and Lord Oxford of the Asquith family. Later Captain Jolliffe married Lady Perdita Asquith, daughter of the ex-Prime Minister. Asquith himself used to come to shoot and was quite a good Shot. In those days we all had a saying: "You have to be like Asquith – wait and see".'

Frank was the only keeper left on the estate during the war. And when Lord Hylton died he was asked to go round with the valuers when they came to assess the estate, as he knew everyone so well and they all trusted him as a go-between. But it resulted in half a million to pay in death duties, so the shooting was cut back along with everything else and Frank's fourteen years on the estate drew to a close.

The butler asked Frank if he would like Lord Hylton's shooting clothes and he gladly accepted. 'What lovely tweeds and hand-knitted stockings they were: they lasted me for many years.'

Thus Frank went as a single-handed keeper to Scotney Castle, Kent, for Mr Hussey, the editor of *Country Life* magazine. He was very particular about the view and hated to see any unnecessary building about. For example, there used to be a lot of hop-pickers' huts and he insisted that these were hidden away in the woods. And he opened the gardens to the public.'

Years later, when Frank returned to look at the estate, he found his old shoot under water, sunk beneath a new reservoir, and he had to be shown round by the boatman on the pleasure lake! The castle had been turned into flats, one of which was taken by Margaret Thatcher. Frank again became a special constable when he moved to Kent and was made sergeant in charge of castle security.

Then Frank went to Ockham Park at Ripley, near Guildford in Surrey. The mansion had housed evacuees during the war and had become almost derelict, and the whole estate was very run down. Felix Fenston bought it, and wanted to establish a first-class shoot there – he had wanted his son to take over but tragically he had been killed in an air crash. Further land there was bought by Charles Hughesdon, who was to develop the shoot with Fenston.

When Frank took over the 2,000-acre (809ha) Ockham shoot there was only a lad to help him, yet they managed to put down some 2,000 pheasants plus 2,000 partridges.

Then Hughesdon sold his piece and the shoot became smaller; and its future seemed seriously in doubt when Fenston died, suddenly and unexpectedly, on the sleeper on his way to the shoot. The shoot did, however, carry on and a new syndicate was formed; it included Frank, who had free shooting in return for his work.

After a few years Mrs Fenston sent for Frank and told him she had decided to let Lord Forte have the shoot – apparently he already owned adjoining land and had been after the shoot for years as he thought it was taking his birds. But after just two years he gave it up and it was let to a builder.

Frank gave up all involvement with the shoot in 1985. It was time to hang up his spurs. He had been a full-time keeper from the age of fourteen till he was seventy – fifty-six years, and even after that he was never far from the sound of guns. He and his wife retired to a quaint old cottage at Ockham Park, said to be the oldest house in Ripley, having previously been a pub and a police station.

On the day before I visited Frank, the eighty-year-old had been knocked off his bike by a passing lorry, but luckily he was not injured. 'Now, if anyone wants me to help 'em out with their moles, rats, mice or bees they're going to have to fetch me.'

The Keeper's Cottage.

HONEST AS THE
DAY'S LONG

───── ○○○○○ ─────

Even Thomas Hardy would have enthused over the unspoilt corner of Dorset where Harry Churchill spent his childhood and discovered the profession which made his family famous. But the country lad who turned his back on book learning and preferred to study the ways of fox and pheasant never dreamed that he would become a TV star in his seventies!

Henry Churchill was born on 7 December 1907 in the tiny village of Turnworth, near Blandford Forum, where his father was keeper to Colonel Parry-Ogden – 'he of the expensive complexion, with a great big red-and-purple nose which was said to be the result of a dog bite'.

Keepering was certainly in the family blood as Harry's grandfather and great-grandfather were keepers, too, as were his father's four brothers, and Harry himself was one of five brothers, four of whom took up the profession.

Harry's first experience of shooting came at the tender age of five, when his father took him to the edge of a wood close to a chalkpit and said: 'You stay here till you're fetched and don't you move'. He was also told that someone would bring him lunch, which consisted of 'half a loaf with a chunk cut out the middle and a lump of butter stuffed inside, and a bottle of lemonade, of course'.

Also that year came Harry's first experience of foxhunting. 'Our house was on the edge of a big wood, where the hounds came drawing through one day. I remember how frightened I was because their tongues were hanging out and I really thought they were going to gobble me up: all quite unnerving and larger than life for a toddler.'

Happier recollections involved the rearing field hut, where the young Churchill would perch on the food sacks listening to the keepers' wondrous tales during their rare moments of rest. He can remember seeing the food boiler full of hens' eggs, 'imported from Poland of all places. The underkeepers used to give us kids a few to eat on the way home, as well as handfuls of the scalded biscuit meal meant for the birds.

'I detested school in those days and would always rather be off bird's-nesting. Not surprisingly, I was always either in the classroom corner with hands on head, or off somewhere. You could be certain that whenever the hounds came round I was off to watch, and I had a good trick to skive off, too – I took bread and marge to school for lunch, and I would chew some up, then spit it out and pretend to be sick. But instead of going home I was straight off hunting.

'I also skived off to go beating. In fact I did it so often that when I went into school the next morning I would sometimes hold out my hand and say "You might as well cane me now".'

Harry's father also worked as a beatkeeper for Lord Eustace Cecil at Lytchett Matravers, Dorset, but left there in 1914 to go back to Turnworth, as a single-handed keeper, after he was declared too old for military service. The war had already started when the family made their adventurous return by double-shaft waggon pulled by two horses.

'Mr Carter, the carter, came and stayed the night and loaded up our few possessions. Our old settee was perched right on the front of the cart and the whole family sat on it, all in a row. On our way we stopped at the Chequers pub, and Mum and Dad went in while us kids stayed put, but they did bring us out one of those large biscuits each, of the kind you could buy anywhere at the time.

'The cottage at Turnworth was on the second-highest point in Dorset, and we had to fetch more horses to get us up the hill. The farmer who helped us had a Jersey herd which produced the most wonderful yellow butter you ever saw. We must have eaten pounds of it between us, with slice after slice of bread. We were all so hungry that day and must have made real pigs of ourselves.

'We were pretty remote at Turnworth and often cut off by snowdrifts. The only thing delivered was a sack of flour brought in by donkey and cart. Mother used to walk seven miles to get the groceries. She used to make such wonderful bread in an oven in the wall. I can still see her now, punching the dough in a big earthenware pot before setting it near the fire to rise. She had a long, flat board to pop the loaves in the oven, and she also made marvellous lardy cakes: you can't buy the like of 'em now. And us kids had to fetch the wood to fire the oven till it was white-hot. What a thirst we used to work up, but there was always a glass of goat's milk available; in fact we were brought up on it.

'It was a wonderful place where we lived, and on a clear day we could see five counties and the Isle of Wight from the cottage. Now our old home near Bulbarrow viewpoint, Ringmore, is just a heap of stones. But we've often been back just to stand on the rubble and remember the good times, which gives us a great deal of satisfaction.

'I can still see the secret places where I played "Indians" and went tracking with the seven boys from next door. This turned out to be excellent training for the Services – no wonder I was to become known as Winston and always called upon to lead! In those early days I could get within ten feet of a roe deer without

it knowing I was there, but what barks of alarm they gave when they did get on to me.

'I was twelve years old when the war finished. What celebrations there were! We were all given a mug each and I can still see the flags waving on all the churches. But despite the euphoria I felt somewhat cheated as I had wanted to play my part in defending the realm.

'Anyway, when I was fourteen, father was a rabbit catcher, having retired from keepering. He also helped on the farm, laying hedges and so on, and I began to assist him. Then Colonel Ogden died and the shoot was let to his son-in-law Devenish, of the brewery family. Walter Shaw came from Norfolk to be headkeeper and lived next door to us.

'Then the estate was sold to Captain Rodd from Devon. Shaw had a lad to help, but he was lazy and got fired, so I was taken on as kennel boy/underkeeper. Gradually I became responsible for improving the partridge population, using the Euston System; I thought the Knebworth System much better, however, using twelve chipped eggs instead of sixteen. We hand-reared the surplus so that they stood a better chance of survival, as did the reduced broods in the care of their parents.

'Then it was all grey partridges, of course. We regarded the redleg as vermin. But in about 1930 Captain Rodd of Turnworth House bought some eggs of the redleg, known to us as Hungarian partridges in those days. These were mixed up with the picked-up greys and distributed over the shoot, the popular idea of the day being to change the blood, but I thought it was a waste of time.

'Our coops were wide apart – twenty-five yards – so that the birds did not congregate, and this gave each covey its own identity. And if I ever caught a pheasant on my partridge beat – boot! – up in the air!

'The feed used was millet, hemp, kibbled maize and kibbled wheat. We fed 'em little and often – as in the wild. But ours was good country and they were getting a lot of natural food, too, especially ants' eggs on old meadow land. We used to spade out the sides of the ants' nests and the birds loved it. The ants bring up their larvae to the heat of the sun, you know.'

Eventually headkeeper Shaw's son left school and Captain Rodd told Harry he would have to make way for the lad, though he could stay on indefinitely until he found another job. Then Harry was accepted for a job simply on the strength of his letter and references.

'I didn't even have to go for an interview. They wanted me to start on the Saturday, but I told them I wanted to play my last game of football in Dorset so I would start on the Monday.'

Thus in 1934 Harry entered the employment of stockbroker Dennis Capron of Southwick Hall, Northamptonshire. After one year Capron took on two more keepers and more land and Harry was put in charge.

'Capron was always interested in the tips we received and used to ask me what I had been given. One day I told him the total was £5 10s for the six guests. "Who gave you the ten shillings?", he demanded. "He'll never shoot here again." And he gave me the ten bob to make up the difference. Mind you, £1 was a good tip then.

'Capron was a real friend to me. I went with him to shoot all over the country, though his valet often did the loading too. One thing I made a point of remembering was where we would get good lunches, and if Capron proposed going somewhere where I knew the food to be poor I used to say "I'm afraid I'll have to stay home tomorrow and send an underkeeper". Us visiting keepers and loaders generally ate in the servants' halls, but we often had the same food as the Guns.

'Mr Capron had a pair of Purdeys and a pair of Holland and Hollands, and always had me carry a huge amount of clobber, including a mac, gannochy, an extra bag with five hundred cartridges and so on, while he sauntered along with only a shooting stick, always wearing a trilby hat. And he was a fidgety sort of chap, constantly changing position and puffing away at Egyptian cigarettes, some of which he gave me. But every time he moved from his allotted peg I had to pick up all the gear and follow, so one day I said to him: "Look here, are you ever going to keep still?" To my great surprise, he simply said: "OK, we'll stop here".

'He was a good Shot – not surprisingly really with all that practice. I had a clicker to record his kills and I remember counting sixty-five to his gun at one stand. Mind you, he was made to look ordinary at Helmsley. There was a top Shot on our left, dealing beautifully with the high pheasants, and no way was he in the same class. Birds were falling so far they split on the rocks. It was cold too. I remember one Gun drooping pheasants' wings over his hands to keep warm between drives on those cold Yorkshire hills.

'Generally, I would say that there are not such good Shots nowadays, as the gentry are not brought up to it like they were, especially as they have such freedom of choice and can travel so easily to do whatever they wish. In the old days a youngster was put in the charge of a keeper from the word go, and I am pleased to say I brought many of them along. I always told 'em they could only shoot in front. Today you see most birds shot up the backside by businessmen not brought up to shoot properly.

'Also, the new Gun's lack of knowledge of quarry can be abysmal. I suppose you know the story about Sir Brian Mountain of Eagle Star. Many years ago, on shooting a woodcock, he is said to have exclaimed: "That's a nice little bird – we must rear more!"

'General understanding of other fieldsports used to be better, too – we all tried to help each other and take an interest. For example, at Southwick we used to have an annual Fox Feast, put on by the Woodland Pytchley for all the people whose land they hunted over. All the keepers attended, and there was very keen competition in the clayshoot.'

In 1939 Harry volunteered for the RAF, determined to play his part after 'missing out' on World War I. He wanted to 'get back at Hitler' and subsequently played a valuable role in ground defence.

He was demobbed in 1945 and spent a year or so working for the Ministry of Agriculture on pest control, vermin having pro-liferated during the war. His main quarry were rats, rabbits and moles, and his best 'bag' was 4,000 rats in one night at Corby refuse dump. 'We had baited the place for two days, and on that third day they were queuing up waiting for the bait.'

With the loss of manpower, there were plenty of jobs to choose from after the war and eventually Harry decided to set-tle down in 1947 as keeper for Major David Watts-Russell on the Biggin Estate, Benefield, Northamptonshire, where he was to spend the rest of his working life.

His great interest in gundogs and field trials began in 1938, when he bought his first bitch, Teal. Sadly, with the war com-ing, he had to sell her, and after the war good dogs were hard to come by. But this did not hold him back and he went on to become one of the most celebrated names on the field trial circuit, having the honour of judging a number of major cham-pionships.

Harry retired from Biggin and full-time keepering in March 1988, at the age of eighty, and even then gave up only because of a troublesome knee – 'It's unfair to continue if you can't do a job 100%.'

However, he remained very active in giving talks to Young Farmers' Clubs, the Women's Institute and other organisations. 'But you have to be selective in what you talk about – nothing too gory for the Girl Guides!' And it was through his ability to present himself enthusiastically and interestingly that Harry came to star in Channel 4's TV special, 'The Shoot', which was very well received.

PUTTING THE QUEEN SECOND

———— ooooo ————

When Tom Walter was presented with a long-service medal at the Game Fair in 1989 he was, of course, honoured to receive it from the Queen, but secretly he was much more excited about meeting someone else. That year the fair was held at Stratfield Saye, the home of the Duke of Wellington, enabling Tom to fulfil a very special ambition. All his life he had wanted to meet His Grace, to tell him about his great-grandfather, who had been gamekeeper to the First Duke of Wellington, the hero of Waterloo, serving Stratfield Saye for fifty-six years.

A kind friend had arranged the meeting and for Tom it could not have come quickly enough. But on the day he was last in a line of ten keepers up for awards. 'The Queen said, "That's a long wait Walter, but now you can meet the duke himself"', and then he stepped forward. It was a fitting tribute to a remarkable career.

Christened Thomas Walter ('There's no s on the end even though everyone calls me Walters') was born on 18 October 1908, at Hurst, near Reading in Berkshire. Surprisingly, neither Tom's father nor grandfather were keepers before him, but he did have a keepering uncle on the Haineshill Estate.

'Granny had four sons, all in the Scots Fusiliers in the Great War. Two came 'ome and two got killed. Father was a foreman bricklayer at only nineteen – now that's a credit! And he was also a wonderful Shot at pigeons. Mother did not work. She was too busy with me and my six brothers and four sisters.'

Tom's earliest memories of shooting are from when he was about twelve. 'We used to go beatin' different places to stand stop. At lunchtime we had lovely salt beef and cheese sandwiches, a bottle of pop and two shillings. The men had five bob.'

He also managed to make a little money from another sport. 'Three of us used to run a rat and sparrow club, when we were teenagers. We went round with clap-nets, all about the 'edges and the ivy on the buildin's. Our torch mesmerised the birds and they were soon caught. We tore their 'eads off and took 'em to the farmers, along with the rats which we used to get when we lifted up the floors on the poultry farms. The farmers had a competition to see who could get the most and the winner was announced at the flower show. We used to kill 400–500 rats a year and gettin' on for a thousand sparrows. We won all four years we entered – got about £4 for the sparrows and £4 for the rats, between the three of us. That was a lot then.

'Years ago there was sparrows everywhere – it was nothin' to get 300 or more in the edge of a wheatfield. We used to get dust shot and if you fired into 'em just right you got dozens. Everyone had sparrow pie then. They pulled the legs out and split the breasts for it. These were the only parts worth keeping. But a lot of the time sparrows were fed to the ferrets which we used to get rats.

'Sparrows are lovely sweet birds, not like a lot of 'em such as the robin and all the tits, which are bitter. With starlings you 'ave to pull their 'eads off and then they are all right. We also used to catch birds such as goldfinches and linnets in the clap-nets, but let them go.'

Tom left school at the age of fourteen to work with his father. 'I think the first thing we did together was build a sectional bungalow, mostly working on the foundations. I always remember this because they had a water diviner to set the well before placing the house.

'In 1925, headkeeper Jim Martin asked me to be his only underkeeper at Bill Hill, near Hurst. My elder brother, who worked in the garden, got twenty-five shillings a week, but I got thirty shillings as I had to work weekends. Mr Martin even arranged with the police for me to carry a gun on the road at seventeen, when it should have been eighteen. The shooting was let to Thomas Haig, the whisky man, and he was my boss – a very nice man.'

At Bill Hill Tom had no special perks, 'but always on the last drive of the year Mr Haig called me out of the woods and gave me a new ten-shilling note. He also said that I would get a bottle of port from Martin. But one of the best tips I ever had was in the thirties. K. V. Peppiat – the chief cashier of the Bank of England – gave me a brand-new pound note. That was a lot then.

'For the older birds in the wood, farmers often used to bring us carcasses and we'd hang 'em up in the trees to get maggots, which would fall out. The pheasants loved scratchin' around for those. As the chicks got older they had Dari seed, buckwheat, hempseed, split peas and groats – that's oats with the husks off, chopped up and kibbled.

'We used to 'ave a bit of fun with the Dari. If you covered a hen's eye and pointed the other at one of the white seeds, and then let her go, she'd stay there mesmerised for some time.

'Poor old Jim Martin had a sad end to his career. When he went to Haineshill he showed somebody where a 500lb bomb had dropped durin' the war. He was standing on the edge of the crater and as he turned round he tripped on some bushes and 'is gun went off and shot 'im in the thigh. People tore up shirts best they could to stop the bleeding and rushed him to Reading hospital, but the leg had to come off. He couldn't work after that.'

After three years at Bill Hill, Tom decided it was time, 'to better meself and apply for various jobs. I could 'ave 'ad the job old Charlie South took at Windsor, but I turned it down as there were too many restrictions. You even 'ad to hand your jacket back if you left because of the buttons with the royal insignia on.

'In those days Crufts was the place to get a job. Old Cruft sold dog biscuits and was really interested in keepers. But anyway, I put an advert in the *Gamekeeper* magazine and 'ad a telegram from Parmore, near Marlow in Buckinghamshire.

'So I cycled up through Henley – about sixteen miles – and got there around 2.30 or 3pm. The Honourable Seddon Cripps, Lord Parmore's elder son, interviewed me in his office. The keeper asked me to start as his second on the Monday, but on Sunday there was about three inches of snow, so I didn't get to Buckinghamshire till about 12 o'clock on me first day. It was a job even to push the bike so I left it halfway. Then I took me case to Skirmett, where the keeper had fixed me up with lodgin's in the council houses.

'The shoot was let to a lovely man – Sir Sydney Sitwell – and there were big plans for it. We 'ad the local carpenter and his son making 250 coops in a barn for us. There were stacks of wood everywhere. The carpenter also fitted out a shepherd's hut with a stove, foldin' table and gauze-fronted larder and I slept in there on the rearing field for four years.

'We 'ad two hermits there. One had 'is hair right down 'is back. He used to get on the bus and people called 'im Jack Frightenem. The other one was called Luxster Jack and 'e came down to the village to get 'is ten-shilling pension and a few groceries each week. He could also catch a rabbit and anythin' to keep 'imself goin'. He made a shack on my beat and the roof was packed with bracken to keep warm. One day the police told me he was dead and they'd had to shoot 'is dog to get at 'im. He was a lovely chap – never hurt anyone.

'Near old Luxster Jack there was a whirly 'ole – one of those springs that bubbles up. If you got a bottle with a cork in and put it out in the middle it would suddenly disappear – *oooosh*. Nobody knew where it went.

'After lunch we only had one drive and would blank in all the 'angin' [hangers – steep hillside woods] for three-quarters of a mile. This took between an hour and one and a half hours and the nine Guns – five in the first line – shot 300–400 pheasants. We always had a policeman with us on shoot day – 'e was paid, of course.'

With such large bags, Tom and his colleagues obviously needed a lot of feed. 'We used to get it by the lorry-load, and the Polish eggs came in crates of 500. I 'ad two boilers for these out in the field.

'Then one day the headkeeper was throwing coconuts at Thame Show and twisted his knee. He told the boss he did it in a rabbit hole, and next shoot 'e sent another keeper in his place, rather than me. The boss said, "Where's Walter?" So I thought – look out for yourself here! It was time to move on. I didn't want to get involved with anyone tellin' lies. I always say tell the truth and you'll never go wrong.

'Anyway, the shoot moved to Ramsbury in Wiltshire and they asked me to go down there. It was run by Thomas Forbes, the insurance broker. But my wife – I married Grace in 1932 – had to stop with Mother till the house was available.'

Ramsbury was in partridge country and Tom operated the old Euston system. 'I wish they'd do it today, we might get the grey partridges back. The idea was to find nests when the birds started to lay, pick up the eggs and put wooden ones in their place. When a clutch got to eleven I stopped putting the dummies in. I always operated in odd numbers because birds can count in twos! I always 'ad a string of eggs with me. Just cut one off and rub it off a bit. They were made by friends – mostly from beech – and were much cheaper than the bought ones.'

While the real eggs were in Tom's care they were safe from predators and sudden weather changes. 'Twenty or so would be set under a broody hen. Then, when they were chipping at twenty-two days or so I put them back in the wild nests. It was always best to get them away before they double-chipped at twenty-three days because they could hatch under your shirt as you walked round. I've carried as many as sixty chipped eggs next to me chest. I 'ad a belt round me so they couldn't drop down. People say to me didn't they die of cold, but they kept quite warm for a surprisingly long time.

'It's a wonderful thing to watch the partridges. You often 'ad to poke 'em off the nest with a stick and I've 'ad them fly up and knock me cap off before. As they were hatching off, the cock would come and sit by the hen to help dry the chicks off.

'At Rambsbury we 'ad this poacher called Monty Fox – and 'e was crafty too. Well, with the partridges my main job was finished by the end of June, so I asked if I could 'ave a few pheasants in the wood – to amuse me. So I did. But the head said, "What shall we do about Monty?" I said, "Just give him a couple of bob extra on beatin' day – at least if 'e's here you know where he is".'

At the time, Tom used to enjoy longnetting. 'That's the way to sweep the rabbits up. One night we had seventy-five. Only thing was you really 'ad to know your ground. Run into a patch of thistles or something and that soon snags you up. We used to go out three or four times a week. Now no one knows the trade. We could 'ave 200 yards of net pegged out in three and a half minutes. Two men would drive in – zigzaggin' – and you 'ad to guess a bit as you might be in front of each other in the dark. A chap took our rabbits to London twice a week and we always looked forward to him comin' round because he brought back lots of fruit, from the market.

'One night, I heard thump, thump, thump. It was the head-keeper kickin' a fox but 'e got out. Worst thing to 'ave in a net was an ol' hare – 'e used to thrash about an' squeal an' frighten everythin' off.

'Another time we started to put the net out when all the rabbits came runnin' by before our men came in. I thought we must be in front of another net – and we were. It was Monty's. So we gave 'im half a dozen rabbits and told 'im to go home and pack it in.

'Monty used to walk through a wood and shoot all the birds on the way back after he'd seen where they were, so that he was in and out as quickly as possible. There was this old tin bath by

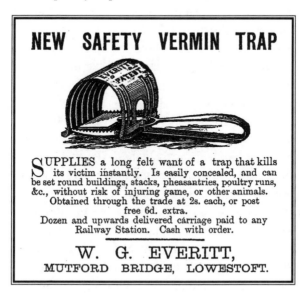

his gate where birds were left for collection, and one day the police was gonna catch 'im. So they got in the shed opposite and waited. Eventually the carrier came by, looked under the bath and out came the police. But there was nothin' there and off they went very disappointed. Half an hour later the carrier's son turned up and then the birds were in place. The thing is, the police shouldn't 'ave blabbed about what they was gonna do.'

In 1936 Forbes warned Tom to start looking for another job because he expected to lose most of his money following a shipping disaster. As a result, through recommendation Tom secured his first single-handed position, for Major Huth at Wansdyke End, Inkpen, near Hungerford.

After a year the major asked Tom if he could do anything about the moles. He replied, 'Yes, but we'll need a lot of traps. So I got ten dozen. Well, you can only catch moles in quantity from the first week in March to mid-April, so this worked in well with my Euston system.

'The major and me used to listen to this series on the wireless about a professional mole catcher. One day he said to me, "Did you hear the professional caught sixty-five moles in a 19-acre field?" I said, "I can beat that – I've caught ninety-two in four days in a 15-acre field".

'Altogether, in Wiltshire I caught about 4,000 moles in five years. One place I would catch four or five in the same trap in one day. They like a damp path best. Twice I've caught two moles in one trap going in opposite directions at the same time. Later on, in Gloucestershire, I caught twenty-two moles, one weasel and one toad in a trap that was never moved. That was in a grass garden path.

'I used to sell the skins to friends for a penny or tuppence. Cock pheasant centre-tail feathers fetched a penny each and a lot of chaps used to slip a few out unnoticed on the big shoots.

Magpie tails and pairs of wings were worth fourpence each and jays' wings about threepence a pair.'

Tom did not have to go to war. 'When it started the major said to me, "When does your age group come up?" I said, "It can't be long as all my six brothers are in it already". He said, "I'll stop that – it's far too much for one family". And he did, bein' an Army man himself.

'We had a rifle range on the estate – right in the corner of Wiltshire and Berkshire – and I looked after it for the Home Guard. The Americans came there too and we used to get a few sticks of Wrigley's spearmint from them. At the same time I carried on with my Euston system.

'There were a lot of interesting guests on the shoot, including the Marquis of Aylesbury from Savernake Forest. He trained fox terriers to find truffles and came over to us with his headkeeper in a chain-driven Trojan car.

'In 1946 the major called me in and asked me to check over his pair of Cogswell & Harrisons, which I always looked after anyway. He told me he was too old to shoot any more and was going to sell the guns back to the makers. He said that if I see another job I should take it, but if I wanted to I could work in the woods.'

That year Tom took a job as single-handed keeper at Adbury Park, near Newbury in Berkshire. 'It was an old family shoot and they didn't care if you only got twenty or thirty a day. I left in 1952 when they was goin' to let the house as a boys' school. I thought, that's no good with boys runnin' all over the place.'

Tom's next stop was Salperton Park, in Gloucestershire, working for the Hulton family – 'the Picture Post people. Dr Zezi, a Harley Street man, looked after the shooting'.

Life at Salperton was quite traumatic for Tom. 'Dangerous! Corr! I remember old man (Sir Edward) Hulton shooting a pheasant on the wall and all the shot came back through me and the beaters. And we had some well-known guests too, including the authors A. G. Street and Macdonald Hastings.

'There was one time Sir Edward was determined to shoot a hare, but we walked all day and he couldn't shoot anythin'. Then I got really fed up, so when 'e fired I fired too and at last we bagged one. He never did know. I didn't want to walk no further.'

After just two years, Tom could not stand Salperton any longer. 'The farm manager didn't like 'untin' and shootin' at all and did everythin' he could to spoil it. He even got a gang of gypsies to camp right by my shoot, when they were supposed to be potato pickin'.'

In 1954 Tom's fortunes changed, when he went to work at Northleach, Gloucestershire, on Colonel Raymond Barrow's Farmington estate. 'He was a proper military man. If 'e said 'e was goin' to pick me up at six it had to be six – not quarter to or quarter past! But he was a lovely man.'

Tom lived and worked on the Farmington Estate for the rest of his days, the first thirty-one years in one house up to his retirement from full-time work in 1985. He never learned to drive or owned a vehicle, but that never stopped him carrying out his duties efficiently. He believed that when you drive about you do not really see what is going on in the countryside.

In everything he did, Tom appeared to be blessed with a sixth sense. 'I suppose it's a gift. If you're out in the woods waitin' for a stoat, suddenly you know it's there even before you look round.

'One evening I was stood by this chap watchin' the pheasants go to roost when suddenly the whole lot got up and flew to the other end of the wood. He said, "There must be someone in there". But I said, "No, somethin's goin' to happen tonight". And sure enough it did – we had five inches of snow. Nature's a wonderful thing, but if you want to know it properly you've got to live with it all the time.'

Unashamedly superstitious, Tom had quite a few unnerving experiences in foretelling events, some extremely sad. 'We 'ad a blackbird used to come out 'ere on the wire and whistle away while my wife was unwell up in the bedroom. Then one day as we were going out my daughter said, "What's that black thing on the ground by the gate? Someone must have dropped a glove." But I knew it was the blackbird and told her to go on. I would pick it up. And my wife died that evening.

'That was four years ago and people say to me, "Don't you ever get lonely?" But I say no – I've been lonely all my life in the woods. And here I've got some wonderful neighbours and friends, as well as a son and daughter who visit me. Also, there's the birds on the nuts all the time. I've had over thirty tits at once.

'But I really miss the birdlife there used to be. We don't get half the numbers now. Down in my woods there was always half a dozen chiffchaffs or willow warblers, but now there's hardly one. And back in Berkshire there were lots of nightingales.'

Tom was obviously very knowledgeable when it came to birds and was lucky enough to find a few rarities in his time. 'The most unusual was a pair of hoopoes – my father saw them too. Another time, in Glouchestershire, there was a foot of snow in the woods and as I walked through all these bits fell down on me. It was a flock of crossbills feeding in the trees above. And I've only once found the nest of a hawfinch. It was halfway up an oak tree on a tuft. You can always tell hawfinches because as they fly along they've got a certain twitter.'

This great knowledge of birdlife was especially useful to Tom in vermin control. 'I don't believe in traps. Only do it if you've got to. If you happen to get took bad no one but you knows where that trap is. I only used the old pole traps and gins when they was legal and there was a very bad case, but I never used poisons.

'You can get everythin' you like if you go at the right time. Always remember that birds of a feather flock together. At one place the carrion crows come four miles to roost in a certain wood – way up in the trees. Only snag is it's a long way home in the dark. Anyway, I put this jackdaw on a fishing line and pulled it in a field where the crows used to gather before goin' up to the roost. By golly, didn't they come down to mob it. I got seventeen the first night. A lot of keepers also used to attract crows with a ferret on a line.

'With magpies too the best thing is to walk about and find their roost. They like a patch of bramble in a big wood. Then you want a good wind and shoot 'em. One place I had sixteen in an evening, and could 'ave got more if I could see in the dark.

'Foxes have never been a big problem. I could call one up anywhere. Once I called two right through me legs! Mating time's always the best because then they've only the one thing on their mind.'

Jackdaws gave Tom a few headaches. 'At Ramsbury they used to get in the pen first thing in the morning and take the pheasants' eggs. One day I was cycling downhill on my way to deal with 'em when a rabbit ran into the spokes of me front wheel and drove the stays of the mudguard up and into my arm as I went over the top. See – I've still got the scars. Mind you, the rabbit came off worse – 'e ended up with a neck a yard long.'

On another occasion Tom was injured by a horse. 'I never liked them much anyway. We were playin' cricket and I went to get the ball when this colt lashed out, split me lip and knocked me senseless.'

But Tom's most serious injury was not at the hands of an animal. 'It was about twelve years ago on the last shoot day that year. I was runnin' through the wood when a bit of nut stick stuck in me eye and snapped off.' At the time Tom did not think too much of it but eventually it caused problems with the sight of both eyes, which he sometimes lost despite several operations.

Fortunately, Tom never been seriously injured by a poacher, but he has helped to nab a few. 'When I was at Inkpen, the nearby keeper at Fosbury, Ronnie Legg, used to hear a few shots before he went off in the morning. I said, "that must be one of your own people as he seems to know exactly when you're around. You want to go off and then come back unexpectedly." So 'e did, and it turned out to be the estate plumber, who was sacked a couple of days later.

'When I was at Adbury Park I new keeper Charlie Maber of Highclere – Lord Carnarvon's castle. He said 'e 'ad someone gets a pheasant occasionally but he didn't know who. I said, "Does anyone come up to see you regularly?" He said, "Yes". Turned out it was 'im too. Whenever this man came over to see Charlie 'e stood 'is gun by a tree and bagged a bird on the way back. You've really got to try to out-think some of these people.'

Inevitably, gypsies were involved in many of the poaching incidents in Tom's day, but they also had their uses – as the providers of magical cures. Perhaps the most bizarre Tom ever encountered was during his time in Buckinghamshire. 'This man 'ad this tapeworm which all the experts just couldn't shift. Then a gypsy told 'im that the only way was to go out next time it was raining to get one of those big, black slugs. Then he had to swallow the slug after puttin' it in salt water to get rid of the slime. It worked all right because I saw the tapeworm in the yard. It must have been thirty or thirty-five feet long.'

Throughout all these adventures, Tom encountered some very severe weather. Not surprisingly, his memories of the bitter winter of 1962–63 remained sharp as Gloucestershire was hard hit. 'One day the colonel said to me, "Let's go and see the snow." So off we went, and there was this coffin stuck in an 'earse. It was there for three weeks. Then there were stranded lorry drivers all over – goodness knows what they did for food.

'The colonel used to ride down on his white horse, Stuffy, to get the village post. And we was forever diggin' people out. Then we got a snowplough for the village. Nowadays, Derek from the farm gets out with it whenever the snow sets in. But some of these people moan, "What's Derek doin' clatterin' about at night?" So I say to them you weren't 'ere in '63. If you 'ad been you'd soon be glad of it.

'One of the worst times of all was the first year of the last war. Everythin' was froze up – even a piece of grass was wide as a board. If you could run you'd catch the hares, the ice was that thick on their backs. Loads of branches, even whole trees, came down with the weight of ice. The milkman never came for three weeks. When I managed to get my shed door open I left it open as I'd never do it again. I went to help the shepherd get 'is sheep and when 'e dropped 'is stick it shot downhill at a terrific rate. And when the sheep was down to the hay you 'ad to watch out – they'd be on top of you they was so hungry. All the rabbit holes were almost frozen right over and the rabbits lived off the chalk – their mouths and teeth were all white.'

Tom Walter died on 3 August 1997.

GOOD TIMES, HARD TIMES

———— ∞∞∞ ————

Snug in her modern suburban home at Alton, Hampshire, Mrs Harry Ward clearly recalled the hard times of keepering life between the wars. 'We used to rely on the money Harry got for skins to buy all the little extras in life, and how well I remember holding the candle for him while he worked away into the night.'

Mrs Ward also vividly remembers how the Duchess of Marlborough used to come to their cottage on the Blenheim estate at Christmas with toys for the children. 'But Harry had to go up to see His Grace to collect his share of beef and baccy. And most of the time we never went anywhere, so when we were occasionally taken in a bus to a Marlborough family event, such as a twenty-first birthday party, it was a real treat.'

Born in prime shooting country, at Deopham, Norfolk, on 9 June 1909, Harry got his first job through the Gamekeepers' Association. At the age of fifteen he followed in his grandfather's (but not his father's) footsteps by joining the profession as kennel boy for the excellent mixed shoot run by a syndicate at Nateby, Lancashire.

After two jobs as a underkeeper, Harry moved to prestigious Blenheim, where his promotion to beatkeeper was a great spur to settling down – this was the year in which he married, 1931. He was to stay there for sixteen years, though from 1940 to 1945 he was with the 117 Regiment, mainly on heavy ack-ack duties in England.

At first, Harry worked for the ninth Duke of Marlborough, a little man generally known as 'Sonny', who 'liked to be called "Your Grace"'. In fact this became quite a joke among all the employees, some of whom impudently used the words 'Your Grace' with unnecessary frequency when addressing their master.

Under Sonny, the keepers' uniform remained very traditional – 'If it was good enough for my father then it's good enough for me', he said on several occasions. So the bowler hats and button-backed coats remained till Sonny's son took over.

Harry recalls that Sonny was a reasonable Shot but 'Lord Carnarvon was less hurried and a nicer Shot altogether'. In fact, it appears that Carnarvon never really liked Sonny, for in his memoirs he wrote:

'Sonny was a pompous little man and I remember one Boxing Day, just as we were finishing breakfast and looking forward to a day's shooting, the butler came in and said, somewhat nervously, "Your Grace, I have a message from your headkeeper to say that he is ill and will not be able to come out shooting today. He wishes to assure Your Grace that he has delegated all his responsibilities to the keeper on the beat and he hopes you will have a good day". Sonny listened in chilly silence which communicated itself to all the guests. He replied: "My compliments to my headkeeper; will you please inform him that the lower orders are never ill".'

In the early years at Blenheim 'there was round-the-clock work for every man'. And Mrs Ward recalled that when they were first married they used to go nightwatching together. 'I was too scared to stay in the house alone and used to sleep on a few sacks while he stood guard.'

Sonny was succeeded by John, the tenth duke, generally known as Bert, and according to Harry 'he was as tall as his father was short'. He was an excellent Shot, but renowned for putting himself in all the best positions. 'For example, as you know, few people are keen to take their turn as walking Gun, and many were most grateful when Bert offered to take their place. But the thing is, we keepers knew that Bert only suggested this when he knew good sport would come his way.

'Bert expected everything to be just so, often quite unreasonably. For example, the way he used to say "hurry up" to his loader Bill Monks, who was the fastest loader I ever saw. Bill was also the Duke's valet, and always drank a pint of beer before breakfast.'

Among other distinguished guests, Harry clearly remembers Winston Churchill, Sonny's cousin. 'He was not really very keen on shooting and always preferred informal days, sometimes on his own. Even then he rapidly grew tired of it and would soon go off painting for an hour or two.'

When Harry first went to Blenheim the beaters were given sandwiches for lunch, but later this was done away with and instead they were given 2s, because of the rationing. 'The keepers and loaders always had soup and Irish stew plus a bottle of light or dark ale, but you had to be quick to get a bottle of brown. And while we joked and ate, the Guns always went to the Palace for lunch.'

In 1947 Harry went to Chawton in Hampshire, as a beatkeeper for Edward Knight, but the shoot was very run down. However, in 1954 the estate was bought by Major Richard Sharples and 45-year-old Harry at last became headkeeper.

Sharples was to be Harry's favourite employer – 'A real toff: quite unlike His Grace, who always wanted you to touch your hat too much.' Later he became Sir Richard Sharples and Governor of Bermuda; a tragic appointment because he was assassinated over there.

Lady Sharples became Harry's employer and later she married Patrick de Lazslo. When he died, Harry worked for his son Damon until retiring in July 1987 (part-time from 1965). He died in 1992, aged 82.

Head-keeper's Lodge, Thirkleby Park.